Your Degrees W n't Keep

You Warm at Night

The Very Smart Brothas Guide

to Dating, Mating, and

Fighting Crime

I

Author's note:

Your Degrees Won't Keep You Warm at Night: The Very Smart Brothas Guide to Dating, Mating, and Fighting Crime is strictly for entertainment purposes, and is not to be used as a substitute for actual counseling and therapy from a licensed practitioner. Also, just in case you were worried, we're pretty sure that no children or farm animals were harmed while writing this book.

Title ID: 3470282
ISBN-13: 978-1453708767
ISBN-10: 1453708766

Introduction

Seven things *Your Degrees Won't Keep You Warm at Night: The Very Smart Brothas Guide to Dating, Mating, and Fighting Crime* isn't, one thing it is, and one thing it could be if you squinted really hard:

1. Even though we've grudgingly accepted this possibility as a byproduct of publishing a relationship book, this isn't a contrived ploy to meet more women. Seriously[1].

Actually, doing something as laborious as writing a book just to meet women is something a Diva Dude would do, and (we think) neither of us are Diva Dudes. (More on Diva Dudes later.)

2. This isn't one of those 200 page long guilt trips written by a couple of scorned former "nice guys" and filled with loads of passive-aggressive antagonism. This also isn't a self-fellating guide on how to be a player or a "Mack".

Although we've both had our share of dating discomfort, we're not bitter or out for justice, and we're not seeking to settle the relationship score. We feel awkward (and a

---

[1] No, really. We're serious.

bit yucky) even writing that, but we felt it had to be said.

3. This isn't one of those relationship books written with the underlying premise that all women are desperately seeking a man. In fact, we're not even targeting any specific gender. Although we understand that women typically make the bulk of relationship book purchases, we've included stuff that's applicable for men, women, and West Virginians.

4. The title should let you know this isn't a book for dummies. There are certain things we're assuming you already know, and we feel like there's no need to rehash or revisit any of them. We wouldn't want to waste our time, your money, and insult our collective intelligence.

Basically, if "Unprotected sex with hookers: Yea or Nay?" is a difficult question for you, this probably isn't the right place for you to be.

5. Although this book is littered with a few subjects and asides unique to the African-American experience, this isn't a book written only for Brothas and Sistas. The desire to be Very Smart is universal, right?

6. This isn't a didactic dissertation, dissecting dating dynamics while delineating the differences between early 20th century courting and current coupling common practices. It's really not that serious. You might actually laugh aloud a few times, and we're perfectly okay with that.

7. This isn't a "How to be in a perfect relationship" book. Although we're definitely Very Smart and admittedly

somewhat arrogant, we're not arrogant enough to believe that two never-been-married before 30 year old guys can possibly possess enough wisdom to create a book detailing how to be in a perfect relationship.

8. With that being said, this is a Very Smart and lighthearted response to some of the questions asked, theories raised, and judgments made by those attempting to navigate the murky waters of the Dating and "New" Relationship Game.

9. Also, we're confident "The Very Smart Brothas Guide to Dating, Mating, and Fighting Crime" will help create a less uptight, more practical, and better educated populace.

Since a "well-informed, practical, and relaxed" populace usually leads to "good relationships," "good relationships" lead to "generally happy people," and "generally happy people" leads to "less crime," you can say that this book is just our attempt to fight crime.

Background

The concept of Very Smart Brothas was first conceived by Johnson D. Riley and Randolph (Kim) Springer, 25-year-old roommates at Muskegee Gentleman's and Industrial Institute in July of 1913. Springer, the self-proclaimed *"ladies man with 50 peanuts in my pocket"* and the introspective Riley would sit in their quaintly pretentious one room shanty for hours on end, dreaming of ways to share their relationship expertise through a mass medium, stuck because the internet wouldn't be invented for another 70 or so years.

Undaunted by their relative lack of technology and the infamous warthog swarms that plagued Arkansas in the summer of '13, Springer and Riley put their heads together to create a list of relationship edicts, eventually transcribing them to paper and posting them on the shanty's copper door. Included were a few revolutionary yet transcendent gems of advice such as *"Bros before Hoes," "Don't shit where you eat,"* and *"Smack it, dammit!!"* Word of mouth quickly spread and Riley and Springer became overnight rockstars, invited to spread their gospel of advice in dormitory shanties throughout the southeast.

Sadly, they both perished in the Great Warthog Smarm Related Fire of 1913, which also destroyed the list as well as most of the warthogs, but their work was already done. The word had been spread. The Champ and Panama Jackson are the present-day manifestation of those lonely shanty nights, where Springer and Riley wrote and argued and theorized for days at a time, burning the midnight oil while ignoring the mad shrieks of the wild warthogs. The men of VSB are here to continue the relationship-related word, to enlighten and excite, to enrage and enthrall, and to educate and entertain. Enjoy.

Contents

(1)
Platonic Schmetonic
Why Platonic Relationships Can't Exist (for the most part)
By The Champ

(9)
She's Just Like Me!
The Art Behind the Frequency of the "Dressed Down"
Approach
By Panama Jackson

(13)
Men, Found in Translation
Decoding and Deciphering the Language of Man
By The Champ

(19)
Love Actually...Sucks
How Movies and Music Can Ruin Real Relationships
By Panama Jackson

(23)
19 Things About Sex I Definitely Didn't Learn in Sex-Ed
By The Champ

(51)
Rate at Your Own Risk
Why Men Should Never, Ever, Ever, Ever Tell a Woman Her
"Score" (Even If She Asks)
By Panama Jackson

(55)
21st Century Chivalry
By The Champ

(63)
The Goggles...
...And Why You Should Take Them Off As Soon As Possible If
You Ever Catch Yourselves Wearing a Pair
By The Champ

(71)
Catching the Running Man
5 Common Things Men Say That Are *Always* Just Us
"Running Game"
By The Champ

(77)
Going Green
A Very Smart Rant from The Champ

(81)
Making Love in the Club...Or Not
21 Tips to Remember When Hitting the Club
By The Champ

(89)
The Tenets of Grown-ass-ness
By The Champ

(97)
Shady Hawkins Day
Why Women Shouldn't Hunt For Men
By The Champ

(101)
Trickeration
How to Get a Date at the Last Minute
(When Being You Hasn't Been Quite Good Enough)
By Panama Jackson

(107)
Salt Your Own Sack
How We (Men) Have Perfected the Fine Art of Being Our Own
Worst Enemy
By The Champ and Panama Jackson

(127)
Friend-Zoned
6 Signs That You've Been Given the "Just a Friend" Title
By The Champ

(133)
Close-Bus Syndrome
Yup, Ladies. Guys Can Put You in the "Friends Zone"
By The Champ and Panama Jackson

(143)
Diva Dudes, Kryptonite Chicks, and Crazy Bastards
The Relationship Jabberwockies
By The Champ

(157)
Dating the 30 Year Old Virgin
A Very Smart Rant from Panama Jackson

(159)
She Really Likes You
A Very Smart Rant from The Champ

(163)
Smiley Face
10 Sure-Fire Ways to Charm a Very Smart Man
By The Champ and Panama Jackson

(169)
Proving My Love
**12 Extremely Painful Things Men Do Only Because They Love
Women**
By The Champ and Panama Jackson

(175)
The Impossible Dream
6 Very Smart Ways to (Try to) Keep Your Woman Happy
By The Champ

(181)
Not So High Fidelity
**Everything You've Ever Wanted to Know About Why (Some)
Men Cheat**
By The Champ and Panama Jackson

(197)
Cheat, Shiiet
A Very Smart Rant from The Champ

(201)
Jazmine Sullivan Might End Your Life
A Very Smart Rant from Panama Jackson

(205)
The Do's and Don'ts of Breaking Up...
...and What to Do If They Don't Get the Hint
By The Champ and Panama Jackson

(213)
Daddy's Girls
Uncut and Unfiltered Relationship Advice We Hope to
Eventually Give Our Daughters
By The Champ and Panama Jackson

(221)
Why I Hate "Good Girl" Problems
A Very Smart Rant from Panama Jackson

(223)
The Cheat Sheet
"Secrets" About Men That We Can't (in Good Conscience) End
the Book Without Telling You
By The Champ and Panama Jackson

(237)
Acknowledgements

Platonic Schmetonic
Why Platonic Relationships Can't Exist (for the most part)

By The Champ

We've heard the story before.

Boy and Girl are both attending annual Delta Sigma Theta kickball game/cancer fundraiser. Boy approaches Girl, and Girl is charmed by Boy's proper use of **eclecticism** *and* **pragmatic** *in a sentence. Boy and Girl exchange numbers, and after a month or so of weekly coffeehouse outings and a trip to Pottery Barn, they become...friends. Not lovers, not even the awkward* **friends with benefits**, *but best friends forever, serving as each others de facto permanent back-up weekend companion, but never, ever crossing that line.*

Sure, they've both seen Chasing Amy[2], and they're both aware that most people don't think that they—two like-aged, attractive, available, and un-asexual people—can stay strictly platonic friends if they stay close to each other. But they're different and they prove their differentness by staying true friends, forever.

Everyone has heard this story before. Everyone has also heard stories about the Lochness Monster, Bigfoot, and light beer that doesn't taste like cat urine, and just like each of these whimsical and completely fabricated ideas, **platonic friendships between men and women do not and cannot exist.**

---

[2] Makes the cut with *Say Anything*, *When Harry Met Sally*, and *The Best Man* on the list of '*The four most awkward movies to watch while in college and sitting on the couch next to your unrequited crush" –The Champ.*

1

Before I continue, I want to make clear that I do believe men and women can be close friends. It's not impossible or even improbable. What I am stating is that the term **platonic** just doesn't fit for several reasons.

Using the strictest definition of platonic—*transcending physical desire and tending toward the purely spiritual or ideal*—like-aged men and women don't just meet each other in situations where physical desire is transcended. We don't actively seek friends of the opposite sex, especially not ones who are close to our age. Millions[3] of years of life on this planet have shown us we're always on the prowl for potential mating partners. Someone (usually the male) has to make the first move and 99% of the time, when we do a cold *"I have no damn clue who you are, but I think you have nice lips"* type of approach on a woman we don't know, friendship is about the last thing on our minds (796 spots below other common initial thoughts such as *"I wonder if she can cook," "Are those real?"* and *"Is that a thong?"*). A friendship may happen, but it definitely wasn't the initial, penis and panties involving plan. Since that's the case, it would be disingenuous to call it platonic. I mean, if you're headed for the McDonald's drive-thru and you accidently smash your finger in your driver-side door, stopping at the emergency room doesn't make you any less hungry, does it? (Don't answer that question.)

With sets of friends where one of them does admit to some romantic attraction but attempts to suppress it for **the sake of the friendship** or some other limp-dicked

---

[3] If you're a Young Earth creationist—a person who staunchly believes that the Earth is only 5,000 years old—just substitute "hundreds" for "millions".
–*T.C.*

bullshit, their relationship, platonically at least, is doomed. Even an inkling of suppressed physical desire has its way of eventually showing itself and both parties are usually aware of its presence, despite how they attempt to deny its existence.

It comes out in the subtle way certain requests made from a woman to her platonic male friend might be accompanied with her voice going up an octave. It also comes out when that same male friend jumps at the opportunity to help her move her 700 pound refrigerator Saturday morning, even though if one of his male friends made that same request, he'd respond with some variant of *"I'm too damn hungover from last night," "I'm so hungover that I cant remember how I hurt my back last night,"* or *"I would but I'm so hungover that I cant find my sweats."*

Plus, even if you claim to be in the 0.1% of people where there's absolutely no romantic feeling harbored by either side in your platonic relationship, you have to figure in **"The Champ's Law of Averages and Percentages,"** which states:

If you willingly spend more than 20% of your free time with someone of the opposite sex, there's at least a 50% chance that at least one of you will develop sexual feelings, or already has developed them but keeps quiet out of fear that they would be unrequited.

X (time percentage)* 2.5 = Y (chance percentage)

According to this equation, if you spend anywhere over **40%** of your free time with a platonic friend, there's

3

anywhere from a **100** to **250%** chance that someone wants to bed somebody.

"Well, what if a guy just isn't attracted to a girl at all? Can't they be friends then? I mean, I'm attractive and all, but I'm sure every guy out there doesn't want to get me into bed."

This question shows that the questioner fails to comprehend one of the first general rules you need to know about men: Generally speaking, **we are very, very, very shallow.** Women would be horrified if they realized exactly how shallow and simple the majority of us are when it comes to sexual attraction. This doesn't make us bad people, but let's just say they'd all be very wise to never underestimate the sheer gluttonous monstrosity of our shallowness. This is important to know because it helps you understand the fact that **no unattached man is going to willingly spend a good amount of his free time with a like-aged woman that he is not attracted to in any way.**[4]

You can't blame this egregious shallowness on us, though. Like I alluded to earlier, our survival as a species is partially predicated on the complex zygomorphic labyrinth men have to process when meeting a new woman. Basically, we'll become extinct if we don't actively attempt to maximize the time we spend around bangable chicks (***bangable***, by the way, is as relative as

---

[4] Why? Well, there are myriad reasons for this, but my favorite is the fact that men are acutely aware of one of the tenets of "Bandwagon Attraction". Basically, we know that our attractiveness score can potentially rise if we're seen out with an attractive woman (*even if we're not romantically involved with her*) because other women will figure that there must be something special about us to warrant her company. *–T.C.*

relative gets), and if you're looking for someone to be mad at about this, blame God.

Sorry ladies, but every male "friend" you have would bed you if the time and opportunity was right. I'm not saying they *want to* but, if they've been single at any point during their relationship with you, you best believe they've *considered it*. Since that "consideration" doesn't exactly mesh with *transcending physical desire*, they're not really platonic. Oh, and don't get your holier-than-thou, *"men truly ain't shit"* panties in a bunch after reading this. Why? Well, just how we (men) have to find something remotely attractive about a woman to willingly spend free time with her, **women don't want to be bothered with straight men who find them (not women in general, just her in particular) completely repulsive.** All that nonsense women talk about wanting to find a straight male friend who harbors absolutely no physical interest or attraction for them is just that...**nonsense.** The dozens of years most women have spent learning how to consciously and subconsciously use their femininity to converse with and coerce the opposite sex leave them ill-equipped to be close with a guy who literally considers her to be like a sister...or brother. I'd show another one of my equations here, but I think you all still need a bit more time to digest the first one.

"How about if we're both in committed relationships, completely faithful to our significant others, and just enjoying each others friendship? That can't work? "

No. But, not so much in the sense that *"it can't work"* as much as *"it will never, ever happen"* Since we've already established men don't seek unattractive women friends while they're single, the only way two people in separate romantic relationships can become truly platonic friends would be if they happened to first meet each other after they both were already in the relationship, an impossibility due to the fact that no man or woman I know is going to be okay with their significant other making *new* close friends of the opposite sex. I don't care how open-minded or trust worthy they might be, it's just one of those things you have to accept is never going to happen, like R Kelly finally going to prison. We just haven't evolved to that point as a species yet. Maybe in 2511, but not now.

Despite all of this, I will say that there are actually four places that exist where a truly platonic relationship *might* work if you happened to meet someone there; paradoxical places where the regular rules of platonic discourse don't apply.

1. A college campus. This works for one reason: If you're living on or around campus, there are literally thousands of like-aged people of the opposite sex living within a 10 block radius of you. You're going to see thousands of the same people over and over again for at least a couple of years, and you can't help but make some real friends after that much continuous close contact. The sheer vast number of people and other romantic options makes the whole *transcending physical desire* thing a real possibility.

I'm also aware that the entire college campus dynamic creates a paradoxical sub-universe where unvoiced or unrequited romantic feelings between friends are bred even more often than the truly platonic friendship, and if you're confused about where you fit in, one very easy question should help you to make that distinction.

6

Would *"you and your platonic buddy"* + *"lonely Saturday night"* + *"romantic comedy marathon"* + *"bottle of pineapple Malibu"* definitely = (quoting Iago from "Othello") **"The beast with two backs?"**

If you answered yes, well, I don't know what to tell you. If platonic friendships were stock, you'd be a bit more Enron than Apple.

2. Online. Online, in this sense, describes people you've met through blogs, message boards, or any other mass communicating medium that attracts like-aged and like-minded people. Being online gives you a veil of security, a pre-screening process where physical and sexual attributes regularly don't come into play. This can allow you to create a friendship based on personal compatibility and common interests without being distracted by child-bearing hips.

With that being said, beware of the deadly and lecherous **Internet Goggles** (More on this later).

3. Work. The work environment has the potential to combine the continuous close contact college dynamic with the like-mindedness of the aforementioned internet connection, a combination that can cultivate a true friendship.

With that being said, beware of the deadly and lecherous **Work Goggles** (More on this later).

4. Your mate's address book. If you're in a relationship, it's actually possible to make new platonic friends if said friends are already friends with your significant other... as long as you don't only befriend the good-looking ones

7

who want to sleep with you. Basically, if you're a man and your girlfriend is BFFs with Beyonce, the only way you can also be BFFs with Bey is if you also befriend her homely homegirl who looks like Drake with a lacefront weave.

You know, I've considered that maybe my platonic friend viewpoint is a bit jaded. This is most likely due to the fact that the one time I tried the very close strictly platonic friend thing, hurt feelings, nasty emails, and some very unplatonic things involving a staircase and a bottle of Moet all eventually occurred within a four year span. Thing is, all that experience did for me is reinforce what millions of years of evolution has taught us; men are simple, women are nuts, and neither of us are equipped for a close and *truly platonic* friendship. The day I'm shown proof of it occurring and succeeding will most likely be the same day I'll show you the Lochness Monster footprints in my back yard.

She's Just Like Me!
The Art Behind the Frequency of the "Dressed Down" Approach

By Panama Jackson

From the impressive *(a heightened sense of smell and taste)* to the annoying *(an inability to parallel park)*, there are a few things about women that transcend age, culture, or station; characteristics most of them have in common with each other. One of the more interesting of these things is the fact that most women seem to assume that we (men) would rather approach a woman when she's dressed down instead of dressed up.

(For clarity's sake, dressed down = without make-up, with a ball cap and sweats, and rocking what has been coined in the Atlanta University Center as the "Spelman College pullback"—just pulling your hair back and putting a rubber band or clamp in place.[5])

And, I have to admit, this assumption is probably true. We do have a tendency to approach women when they're not looking their best, but not for the reasons most women assume. It really isn't that we don't care how women look, although there's definitely a school of men out there who could care less what you look like as long

---

[5] This look ranks just behind the **"seated arched back stretch/yawn"** on the *"Sexiest non-sexual things that a woman can possibly do"* list. Seriously, there's sexy, there's very sexy, and there's *"seeing a woman sitting down somewhere studying and watching her do the extended yawn/stretch where she extends her arms and arches her back so much that her sweater lifts and shows a bit of back skin"* sexy. That shit is so sexy that I'm honestly surprised that The Reality Kings or some other internet porn company still hasn't started a series called *"Sexy Seated Stretching Sistas"* yet. —*T.C.*

9

as you are breathing. Even then, there's a school of men out there who don't even care about that.

Women tend to be dressed down when they are going to the grocery store, class, Target, the dentist's office, or any other place where getting dressed up just really doesn't make any damn sense. What makes these venues so approach-friendly is that they're all places where we can find some sort of common ground and even a valid reason to speak. If I'm sitting next to you in class, I can think of a reason to speak to you. If I'm in Target, I can for damn sure find a way to get close to you and find a reason to speak to you.

Setting: Kitchen cleaning/Nerf football aisle in Target

Pimpin' Panama: *"Excuse me... I'm just wondering, would you suggest that I go with this Comet or the off-brand stuff with what looks to be a picture of Morgan Freeman at some southern prison on the label?"*

Potential Playmate: *"Umm... I'd get the Comet myself, but that's just me."*

Pimpin' Panama: *"Hey, thanks. I really do appreciate your help here. Girl, why are we fakin'? You know you want me, girl give me your number... forget it, here goes my number... forget it, you don't need my number because we're gonna get hot tonight!"*

Of course, that isn't exactly what would be said. But, for the sake of this theory and the fact that most dudes come at women wrong anyway, I thought I'd end the saga like that. But, the key is: **Location. Location. Location.** How she's actually dressed is irrelevant because beauty (and booty) transcends everything she might be doing to intentionally downplay her looks.

Also, aside from polygamists and lesbian car thieves, most women don't go grocery shopping in groups. Why is this important?

Scientific Fact: *A man's chances of getting somewhere with a woman are inversely proportional to the number of people around her. The more women around, the less chance he has of getting a smile or a number.*

It doesn't matter if it's a supermarket aisle, your sister's cookout, or a soup kitchen (*Hey! Soup kitchens are great places to meet people. Don't knock it until you've tried it*), if she (*Potential Playmate*) has her girls around, he (*Pimpin Panama*) will probably reconsider his approach for fear of getting humiliated. She doesn't have to be nice because her friends can make you feel like an asshole for her. I'm not saying it's an automatic that she'll be a bit of a dick, but the more people around, the more likely a person may dickishly act out of character. If she's alone, however, she's less likely to be rude and she'll probably just politely decline if not interested.

Why is this important? **Witnesses!** If it's just him and her and he sees her out somewhere again—*after she made him feel like an idiot*—it's his word against hers! If he got rejected and nobody was around to see it, did it really happen? Maybe. Maybe not. He has nothing to lose this way. He can spit his "D" game and it's okay because nobody can verify it ever actually happened. Women tend to be alone when they are dressed down, leading to the fact that there are (*drumroll please*)...**No Witnesses.**

11

Quick story: I managed a Washington, D.C. area nightclub a couple of years ago. In that time I saw many absolutely breathtaking women, women who I felt were completely out of my league. But, where did I usually see them? The blocked off VIP section, sitting next to *Insert Rapper/Professional Athlete/Reality Television Star/SuperStar Blogger Here*. At that point, I felt that I didn't have a realistic shot because, well, these women looked like they should be starring as Janet Jackson's baby sister in *Tyler Perry's Why Did I Get Married, For*.

But, let me catch her slipping at the convenience store, looking like us commoners/regulars. At that point, we're on the same level and we might even be in the same aisle. It goes back to the witnesses point: I have nothing to lose by talking to her because maybe it didn't really happen! It's basic barbershop psychology. At the store, she's **Just Like Me.** Under these circumstances, I have no reason not to approach her because she's dressed down looking like everyone else in the grocery store (just a regular person, not a video vixen), but finer!

And, because I love her so much, I'm going to call this **The Patti LaBelle Theory**. She sang *"On My Own"* which is how you can catch most women slippin': **Dressed down, in the grocery store, all on her own.**

Men, Found in Translation
Decoding and Deciphering the Language of Man

By The Champ

Ladies, before continuing your Very Smart journey to relationship bliss, pay close attention to these scientific interpretations and translations of some of the most common phrases communicated between the sexes.

You say: "Do you like my new hairdo?"

He hears: "Since you haven't said anything about my new hairdo yet, I'm assuming you hate it. But, if you say you like it now, I'll know you're lying. Basically, you're fucked."

He says: "Hey, I just wanted to tell you that I care about you, and I think about you all the time."

He means: "I know that I'm a half-thread of toilet paper on the anal fissure of bad boyfriends, but I'm hoping this'll make you verklempt enough to forget that and continue the daily blow jobs."

You say: "We need to talk...later."

He hears: "You know you done fucked up, right? But, although I know what I need to talk *at you* about will probably take less than five minutes, I'm just going to let you linger in anticipation for the rest of the day for the upcoming guilt-ridden tongue-lashing you're going to receive about something you still have no idea you even did."

13

He says: "That's not what I meant."

He means: "Actually, I did mean exactly that. But, since this unexpectedly upset you, I'm going to continue to rephrase it until I find something that works. Take a seat. This might take a while."

He says: "Huh? Excuse me? Can you repeat that?"

He means: "I heard you, but I just need a bit more time to patch up this tattered story."

You say: "What's your name?"

He hears: "I want your babies."[6]

You say: "I usually get along with men much better than I get along with women."

He hears: "I'm a ho. No, seriously. I've held more wangs than a Chinese cemetery."

He says: "I really don't understand women."

He means: "I really don't understand why women generally think I'm lame."

He says: "Are those real?"

---

[6] Admittedly, if she's from Cincinnati, Ohio, this is probably true. Seriously, I've been to 40 different states, 4 different countries and 2 different continents, but women from Cincinnati are easily the most sexually forward. Just thinking about the things I saw at Club Ritz and Annie's a few years ago makes the Bible I keep on my dresser catch fire. Basically, it's the most underrated place on Earth to have a bachelor party. –T.C.

He means: "Are those real? I don't care either way. I'm just curious."

You say: "I'm not really that hungry right now. What are you in the mood for?"

He hears: "Even though I said I'm not that hungry, I'm probably going to shoot down your first three suggestions. My advice? Pick a restaurant without pictures on the menu."

He says: "Where did you learn how to do that?"

He means: "Seriously, where did you learn how to do that, how crazy must you be to have that skill-set and still be single, and will you marry me??? "

You say: "I have a boyfriend"[7]

He hears: Either "Try harder" or "No offense, but I think you're a homosexual." No in-between.

He says: "Don't worry about dinner tomorrow."

---

[7] Ladies, if you're at the club and you want to get that toothless dude with the 8 button leather zoot suit and the cup of Hen-Rock to stop talking to you and "I have a boyfriend" doesn't work, try one of the following:

1. Tell him you have an STD (unless he already has one and thinks a second one might cancel it out).
2. Ask him if he's holding any crack on him (nobody wants to date a crackhead, unless of course it's Bobby Brown that's hitting on you).
3. Tell him you used to be a man (this should only be attempted if all other options fail) –*Panama Jackson*

He means: "Since I'm making dinner tomorrow, this means that I'm off the hook for another five months, right?"

You say: "I miss you."

He hears: "Bastard, if you don't at least tell me that you miss me back, we're probably not having sex again until the Cleveland Browns win another game."

He says: "I miss you, too."

He means: "I actually do miss you. Well, at least certain parts of you, but not enough to actually tell you first. I'm just saying this because I don't want you to feel awkward."

You say: "I have a really attractive friend who'd be great for you."

He hears: "My friend has eight cats. Five of them are better looking than she is. And, according to her last boyfriend, one of them is actually better in bed."

He says: "What's your friend's name?"

He means: "Is there a clause for buyer's remorse in our relationship contract?"

You say: "Do you think she's attractive?"

He hears: "I need to know which types of women you find attractive so I can start hating them for no apparent reason. I'll also need this info to limit your contact with any of my girlfriends who might favor them."

He says: "Am I getting fat?"

He means: "I'm gay."

He says: "We should work out together."

He means: "I like you. I really do. But, I'm going to make your life a passive-aggressive living hell until you lose some weight."

He says: "I'm not looking for a relationship right now."

He means: "I'm not looking for a relationship with you right now...just your vagina."

You say (if you're his girlfriend) "I'm going out with my girls tonight."

He hears: "I'm going to go out, flirt with a ton of men, accept a bunch of free drinks, dance with my girls, grind with a couple guys like an extra in a Freekey Zekey[8] video, and come home and take out all of my drunken sexual energy on you. I might also cheat on you. And, I just might do both. By the way, the decision I'll make has already been determined."

He says: "When was the last time you had sex?"

---

[8] For those unaware of who is he, Ezekiel "Freekey Zekey" Jiles is the least talented member of the Dipset, the most ignant and least talented popular rap clique in New York City; a place which has been producing the least talented rappers in Hip-Hop for the last 10 years. He's also business partners with second most untalented member of the Dipset, Jim Jones, a man who also happens to be my personal nemesis (even though he's probably completely unaware of this fact). –T.C.

He means: "If we do the do and I decide to go down on you, I won't taste Gerald's nuts, will I?"

You say: "How was your day?"

He hears "Did anything happen to you today that I can somehow segue into a 17 minute tangent about myself?"

He says: "My day was good. Yours?"

He means: "Even though this never works, I'm begging you to allow my blatantly succinct answers to rub off on you."

He says (to a girlfriend): "Hi."

He means: "What's wrong???"

He says: "What's wrong?"

He means: "What did I do???"

He says "What did I do???"

He means: "I know exactly what I did; I just want to see how much mileage and left over fuel perks I still have on this ignorance card."

Love Actually...Sucks
How Movies and Music Can Ruin Real Relationships

By Panama Jackson

Love Actually is one of my favorite movies of all time. For those unfamiliar with the plot, it's a British romantic comedy revolving around the lives of 10 interconnected couples, and their accompanying "love stories." Yeah, yeah, yeah, I know it's kind of gay.[9] (*Not that there's anything wrong with being gay. Shit, my best friend has at least one gay cousin.*) You'd assume that a gangsta like me would only be into uber-gangsta movies like *Shrek, The Lion King, or Beethoven's Second*. But, gangstas love British humor too, and I probably watch this movie at least once a month.

After my 118th or so viewing, though, I've come to realize that if hip-hop is ruining the Black community, movies like this are exactly what are wrong with

---

[9]On the spectrum of "Things some straight black men regularly do that have obvious homosexual undertones," publicly admitting to loving movies like *Love Actually* scores a 12.8%, definitely "unstraight," but not as unstraight as **"Intentionally sagging your pants" (77.4%)**, **"Being violently homophobic" (98.7)**, and **"Running a train."**

Actually, there's a very user-friendly equation to figure the amount of inherent unstraightness with a guy's position in a train.

(p (number of guys involved) * q (your position on the train)) * 5.8

Basically, if you're running a train with five other guys and you're third up to bat, you've officially committed an act that was 104.4% unstraight. Sorry fellas. −*T.C.*

relationships. See, these movies make us believers in love and pandas and all that's wonderful and right in the world. *Love Actually* is just...*inspirational!* I start believing in the possibilities. When it ends, it makes me want to do something nice for any of the women in my life. Shoot, one time, I called my momma after watching it just to tell her I loved her. Don't worry though. Shortly thereafter, I went out and robbed two old ladies and kicked a squirrel into oncoming traffic to maintain my gangsta.

But, it's a movie for a reason. The people who wrote it created it because they wanted to see love and happiness on screen. And, since they have to go home to their husbands and wives and other loved ones who've caused them to seriously consider murder at least once or twice, this makes perfect sense.

Music is exactly like that as well. There are so many great love songs that make you *believe*. And that's great...except its only part of the story. We all believe in the hour and thirty minute screen version of love or the three and a half minute long radio version and want that. We forget about the insecurities, situations, and experiences that won't let us love the way they do in the movies or the way crooners sing in the studio.

We hope, pray, and dream for the beautiful love and happy endings that we see or hear. But, then the song ends, the credits roll, we change the CD, we go home, and we're pissed because our significant others don't make us feel like that anymore.

We loved Jodeci so much that we forget that K.C. Hailey was an actual crackhead[10], and we all know that crackheads can only love the pipe.

There was a time when you had the **thunderbolt** and seeing that certain person gave you butterflies and made your heart skip a beat. But, one day, you noticed all the butterflies had flown away, and you couldn't understand why. The people in the movies seemed to always have them, so why shouldn't you? Then, you get into arguments because you don't understand how your loved one can always forget to do those little things. In the movies, they do the little things. Birthdays are never forgotten, the toilet seat is always down, no one is ever too tired to cuddle, and the wet spot doesn't exist. We forget that they're actors and actresses reading a script and being directed; actors and actresses who occasionally have screwed up lives of their own. But, that doesn't matter because they made us happy.

And that's exactly how the media screws up relationships. It gives us hope and belief in love without telling us how to get over our own insecurities about love and romance. Even the worst case scenario, as occurs in *Love Actually*, made me believe that sometimes love can

---

[10] **The three most influential black crackheads of the modern era?**

1. DeVante Swing. Not only is he the music behind Jodeci, he also gave us Timbaland, Missy Elliot, and Ginuwine. By the way, am I the only one who wonders if Dalvin harbored resentment for not having his name included in JoDeCi?
2. Marion Barry. No explanation needed.
3. Bobby Brown/Whitney Houston. I'm including them as one because I really don't know who introduced who to what. I just know they were both on that rock at one point. –*P.J.*

trump all and make somebody work through the rough times. The only problem with that is the assumption that *love actually* is there in the first place.

So, the next time you go to the movies to see a romantic comedy, remember that reality can suck if you're only prepared for the *movie parts*. And, that favorite on-screen couple you're always comparing and contrasting your relationships to? He's a professional actor, she's a professional actress, their lines were written by a professional screenwriter, their love scenes were crafted by a professional director, and their smoldering chemistry is a direct result of a particularly good casting director. Not only are the characters not real, in real life your favorite "couple" have probably each been divorced once, sued for libel twice, and have had their mug shots on The Smoking Gun thrice.

And, if this doesn't work, just start watching porn. At least you might learn something that's actually helpful.

19 Things About Sex I Definitely Didn't Learn in Sex-Ed

By The Champ

We're all family here, right? I'm reminding myself of this because I'm about to admit something somewhat disturbing, and I'm scared. But, since you all have already proved you trust me by purchasing the book, I should do something to prove this trust is reciprocal, right? Okay, here it goes.

As a grown man, I've felt that I *should be* an expert by now on the female orgasm; a virtual "make-her-cum" maven, if you will. In my lifetime, I've (hopefully) seen a number of them, and (hope that) I've been a very active part in inducing most of them. **But, if I were coaching a sex team (bare with me) and was asked by my players to diagram a female orgasm play for a sure and easy touchdown, I'd be utterly clueless,** and this deeply saddens me.

But, the fact that many women don't seem to know a ton about their own orgasms either makes me feel a little bit better. Don't believe me?

Go to any women's magazine or relationship website and read the numerous comments made and articles from 25 to 40 year old women who've never even had one before. Check out the numerous published scientific studies devoted to the "mysterious" female orgasm, and then check out how many of these studies have contradictory findings. Ask a typical woman how many uncontrollable variables matter when having the big O. I've even heard

23

one woman say she couldn't climax unless it was between 62 and 67 degrees, a fact which really limits honeymoon options.

I'm not saying that men should stop trying, but finding out that many women don't even know exactly how to get themselves off takes a bit of performance pressure off of us. I don't feel so bad about relying on Hail Mary passes to score anymore.

Anyway, this *"nobody knows shit about the female orgasm, women included"* is the most prominent of the many things I've learned about sex since becoming an adult. What else have I learned? Glad you asked...

1. Women have many ways of subtly letting you know they want to sleep with you. Because many, if not most, American women have been socialized to not make their sexual wants and desires easily known, it practically takes an expert in subtle sign reading to know if she's definitely ready to go. This is especially true with "decent" raised-in-the-church, HBCU attending black women, many of whom would sooner die than actually tell a guy, *"Hey, I just wanted to let you know that I would like to have sweaty, matrix, monkey sex with you tonight. I hope you don't mind."*

When you combine this with the fact that most men aren't sign reading savants, you can see how sexual signs are regularly misinterpreted and misread. But, as I've learned, there are more than a few somewhat subtle signs that she's just waiting for you to make a move so she can mount your Everest.

A) It's after 9 pm, she invites you to her place, and she's dressed as if she's auditioning for a spot on the Panamanian women's cricket team.[11] Every woman has *"comfortable house clothes that look like she's about to run to the store or do some laundry."* Every woman also has *"comfortable house clothes that look like she's about to film a scene for Penthouse Pet Pilates."*

Basically, if absolutely nothing, not even a chicken bone or a swallow of Kool-Aid, is left for the imagination and you can **easily see** that you've reached the *"Underwear optional"* portion of the relationship, it might be time to crack that bottle of Cialis.

B) You're alone with her and she pours herself another glass...*and another...and another.* Her doing this can indirectly suggest four completely separate things:

I. She feels safe enough around you to not only be tipsy, *but have you be fully aware of her tipsy-ness.* (This is usually a great sign.)

II. She's giving herself the *"Okay...stop being nervous. We're gonna do this tonight and it's gonna be great."* pep talk. (This is usually a good sign.)

---

[11] I can imagine a few people are wondering why dressing like a member of the Panamanian women's cricket team is so different from, I don't know, dressing like a member of the American women's cricket team. If you are one of those people, I strongly encourage you to Google "Panamanian women's cricket team" so you'll see exactly what I'm talking about. – *T.C.*

III. She's giving herself the *"Okay, I know he's not that attractive and he smells like spider webs, but I'm horny, and, well, I'm horny, and that's that."* pep talk. (Although it could be better, this isn't a terrible sign. You can at least give yourself props for picking a horny one.)

IV. She's a lush. (This is a terrible sign…unless, of course, you're also a lush. In this case, she might be your soul mate.)

Either way, it's a flashing yellow light, so slow down, look both ways, record it with your iPhone so you don't get charged with date rape, and go!

Actually, to be honest, the Very Smart move to do in this situation is just leave, because her being tipsy during your first time opens up a can of moral and legal worms that can make a huge mess. Plus, where's the fun in saying *"Say my name"* during sex if she's too drunk to even remember it?

C) She asks about your sexual history. While it's true that sexual histories should always be discussed before a new couple decides to sleep with each other for the first time, it's also true that these questions won't be asked unless she's seriously considering sleeping with you. In fact, she's already there. Most women aren't going to bring up a subject that implies a sexual future between you two unless she's already made up her mind, and asking those questions is her way of saying *"Okay, unless you tell me that you're a retired porn star or my long lost nephew, we're probably going to have sex in the near future."*

D) She makes excuses to touch and get close to you. From her complaining about being cold while you're both watching *Love, Sex, and Eating the Bones* while sitting on the couch in your hot ass apartment, to her suggesting that you take a Samba class together on your next date, women have myriad ways of saying *"I want to be next to you"* without actually saying it, and this usually means the roll in the hay isn't too far away.

Personally, my favorite is the *"Dormitory Aphrodisiac"*— her engaging you in a *"my masseuse skills are better than yours"* argument just so you can give each other the *"I just want to see how much skin they allow me to touch"* late-night back/chest massage.

With that being said, I'd be remiss if I didn't remind you all that there are evil women out there intent on teasing the entire male populace into oblivion; women who'll intentionally do everything in their power to ensure that all men's balls are bluer than the Arctic Ocean. If I were president for a day, after I absolved all college credit-card debt, I'd pass a bill making sure that every intentional cocktease was forced to wear a sweater with a giant red "CT" like Hester Prynne.

2. Forget about immediate sexual compatibility. What really matters is *libido* compatibility. From barbershop and locker room conversations to songs like Missy Elliot's "One Minute Man", the idea that wack sex with a person would never get better was repeatedly engrained in the head of the young Champ. Basically, if you didn't have great sex the first time, it was never going to happen, and this is probably due to a physical or mental issue that could never be changed. While this may be true in some extreme cases, most couples can grow to be more sexually compatible, and every person has the opportunity to get better in bed.

Thing is, while there's a lid for every pot, some pots require a bit more time on the stove than others. Even the happiest and strongest coupling will eventually shift to shit if one party is cool doing it with once every other week or month or so and the other needs it at least once a day. Eventually, one of them will have to compromise a bit more than the other. And, depending on who does the compromising, this always results in either the low-libidoed person feeling used for sex and eventually hating it, or the high-libidoed one feeling unwanted and eventually resenting their mate.

3. Being completely "Sprung" usually isn't a good thing. It usually sneaks up on us. One day, you're minding your own business, daydreaming about crocheting and pears and what to wear to single's bowling night. Then, 48 hours later, your body has become an erogenous minefield; a walking, incoherently talking victim of PTFS (Post-Traumatic Fuck Syndrome), and you're wondering to yourself, *what the hell just happened and when the hell am I getting some again?*

Here are a few signs that you might be hopelessly stuck on the springboard.

A) You become Flavor Flav. I lived in a corner suite— two bedrooms separated by a common room area—with three other roommates my freshman year of college, a somewhat unremarkable arrangement sans for an entertaining bi-monthly occurrence the entire second semester. One of my roommates (Jay) had a regular fuck-buddy (Kimmie), an extremely demure sophomore who would come through every other Saturday afternoon (*Yes. Afternoon!!! Who has Saturday afternoon booty* *calls???)*, chop it up with us in the living room for a few minutes while we were playing NBA Live, then head to the bedroom with Jay.

Dormitory walls are notoriously thin, a fact making afternoon sex a community affair. This obviously didn't faze Kimmie at all, though. Without fail, within fifteen minutes, the barely audible moaning would begin. Nothing unusual there though; just your garden variety sex moans. Soon though, the moans would then give way to **the words.** By "*the words*" I mean that when Kimmie was kumming, she'd scream out some of the most bewildering, befuddling, and *hilarious* word combinations known to man. From "*You're punching it Papichulo*" to something that sounded like "*fuckkkkk!! toaster!! fuckkkkk!! toaster!! fuckkkkk!! toaster!!*" she'd use horrifically awkward syntax, with word combinations sounding similar to something you might overhear at in an ESL classroom for toddlers with Tourette's. Afterwards, she'd come back out with us and play spades or tonk like nothing happened. In hindsight, I probably should have married Kimmie.

My point is there's sex, good sex, very good sex, and sex that'll have you doing and saying the most inane and unbelievable shit during and directly after the act. The type of sex that'll make you jump up right afterward and iron clothes butt naked at 3 in the morning while whistling the instrumental to John Legend's "Ordinary People." Nothing you do during or directly after that time can be explained by any type of rational thought or reasoning. Basically, you become Flavor Flav.

B) You schedule important shit *around* sex. *"You know, even though I don't have any gas in my truck, and stopping*

29

for gas will ensure I wont have any cash to buy lunch today, I need to drive to work instead of catching the bus today, just to give me those extra 15 minutes I need this morning to play another round of 'Catch The Bed Burglar' with my baby before I get up and take a shower. Wait. Whoa. How did she fit the entire thing in her mouth, and why am I squealing like a pig?? I didn't even know I could make that noise. You know what? Fuck work. I'm just going to call off."

These are the types of conversations you have with yourself ***everyday*** when you're on the springboard.

C) You're willing to overlook common sense deal-breakers. *"She still lives with her mom? So what? Stop hating. She has the whole basement to herself anyway."*

"He has a different colored faux-gold grill for each season? Well…you can't really tell in the dark."

"Her baby daddy is Kimbo Slice? Whatever. That bald nigga can't beat me."

Most of us have been there before, where you're so into someone that you always find yourself making excuses for them and intentionally ignoring shit, instead of actually wondering why you're always making excuses and ignoring shit. This—the fact that your cognitive sense goes completely to shit—is easily the worst byproduct of the springboard. On a positive note, the antagonists in these types of situations have been the muses for some of the best music, movies, and art ever made, so maybe it's not all bad.

4. "Performance" porn sex (stupid acrobatics, stupidly awkward positions, sex in stupidly random places, stupidly

adding people to the sack, etc.) is usually pointless, awkward, and painful if performed by non-professionals. Quick story: During my sophomore year of college, a few teammates and I were so consumed with hotel jacuzzi sex that we had an on-going bet with each other about who would do it first. Although I lost the bet, I eventually did the deed a few years later, and spent the entire time underwhelmed by the feeling, annoyed with the chick trying not to get her hair too wet, and irritated by the chlorine-filled water splashing up my nose and in my eyes. Moral of the story: Don't watch *Showgirls*.

5. Don't trust a person who says they never masturbate. If they're lying, they're too anal and pedestrian to realize that they're not in high school anymore and it's not a subject worth lying about. If they're actually telling the truth, they're future murderers.

Obviously, I have extremely positive feelings about masturbation and how productive it can be, and here's why you should too.

A) It's great for vagina vetting. *No sense of humor. A warped sense of self. Smells exactly how Courtney Love looks.* These are just a few of the many qualities widely considered to be immediate deal breakers, yet each of these pale in comparison to the horror exhibited when encountering a grown-ass woman who proudly states that she doesn't masturbate.

Usually when making this claim, they'll happily follow up with some variant of *"I mean, why I would do something like that when I can just call someone do to it for me"*, a statement which basically advertises...

31

"Hey everyone! Guess what?? I have a barren and stupid crotch. I also wear jeans to bed occasionally and I keep a fridge full of Dad's root beer."

B) It's a useful form of kitten control. Kittens, with their big eyes, playful dispositions, adorable whiskers, and furry feet are the bane of human existence, stealth mammal spies sent from the devil to steal all of our belts and murder Dave Chappelle. As a part of VSB's crime-fighting ideals, I won't stand idle while we allow these cute-ass beasts of prey to destroy our quality of life. Because of this, I try to kill at least two kittens per day. It's the least I can do.

C) Yup. We're talking about "Practice". When you buy your AK-47's, you don't just start immediately and indiscriminately spraying up your block and harassing co-workers do you? No, you go to the firing range to practice first. Why? Because even though you own your gun, you don't *know* your gun. Maybe your gun has a light trigger-pull, and it doesn't take much stimulation to fire. Maybe your weapon needs to heat up a bit before it's able to shoot accurately. Maybe you need to practice your aim, because maybe your gun isn't as powerful as you thought it was, so your ass better be an expert marksman. Since going through life with the least amount of maybes possible helps to fight crime, doesn't it make sense to practice a bit before *(and after)* the big game? You can never have too much practice. I love practice. Sometimes during a game, I'll be thinking to myself, *"Self, I can't wait until I get an opportunity to practice this some more!"*

D) It's the ultimate multi-tasking test. Let's just say that once you're able to effectively type one-handed coherent, legible, and intelligent thoughts to a client on your blackberry *while popping the Pepsi can[12]*, there's nothing left to accomplish as a human being.

E) Procrasturbating gets you closer to God. Loosely defined as what occurs when you masturbate to alleviate boredom, ***procrasturbation*** ensures that you're actually doing something with those idle hands and thoughts instead of letting the devil take over. So, the next time you're asked to explain what you were doing between 6:00 and 6:15 that was so important that you couldn't answer your phone, just say you were getting in touch with God.

6. A woman can actually fuck her way into a man's heart, but she needs to have sex with him at least a couple hundred (thousand) times to do it. The scenario usually unfolds the exact same way:

Guy meets Girl. Girl is digging Guy, and Guy is digging Girl just enough to sleep with her but not enough to actually commit to her. Girl reluctantly accepts deal and begins a relationship with Guy where they see each other between 1am and 4am three nights a week. Occasionally Girl and Guy extend time to 5am to eat cereal and watch Seinfeld reruns together. This process repeats on and off for 18 months, until Guy asks Girl one day if she would like to go to Wendy's together...in the day time. Girl accepts offer, and Guy and Girl live happily ever after.

Although the common cliché is that men can have perpetual emotion-less and feeling-less sex, even the

---

[12] I have many extremely crude and extremely immature euphemisms for female masturbation. This one just happens to be my favorite– *T.C.*

33

coldest cat can't continue to have sex with a person over and over and over again without developing some feelings for them. Thing is, "over and over and over again" might have to be 350 times for it to actually start working.

7. There actually are women who are able to "date and fuck like a man" (read: "have perpetual emotion-less and feeling-less sex")...and these women are to be avoided like the swine flu.

8. There aren't many moments more awkward than letting someone you care about know that they suck in the sack. Because of this, many people tend to just avoid the awkwardness altogether, resulting in tons of terrible sex having people walking the planet, completely oblivious to the plague of pathetic punany and pauperized pumpage they're exposing to an unsuspecting populace. Luckily, as I'll discuss later in this chapter, this problem is easily correctable. But, before any improvements are made, the issue has to be recognized and acknowledged, and here's how you can tell that you just might suck in the sack.

A) You have the *Tragic* Stick. Put it this way, Casanova, if your sex life personally remixes the chorus to 50 Cent's "Magic Stick" from...

"I know if I can hit once, I can hit twice"

...to

"I know that I can hit once. Twice? Eh. Good question"

...then maybe you should substitute *"Who's your daddy?"* and *"Say my name"* for *"This is really great. Thank you for the opportunity"* and *"Do you want a check or cash?"*

While being able to sleep with someone repeatedly is far from a concrete indictor of sexual prowess and performance, there's usually a real reason why your pilots never get picked up for syndication. You just have to figure out if it's the stars or the script before your idea gets dumped permanently.

B) The usual courteous post-coital warm and slightly damp clean-up towel has been replaced by a box of Kleenex frisbeed at your head. From what I've heard, constant visible visceral frustration at your performance usually isn't a good thing.

C) He never plays the "Poke Game" For men, the relentless pursuit of the possibility of morning sex is embedded in our DNA.

From accidentally letting it slip out of our boxers and rub our women's behind to our perfunctory half-asleep nonchalant **"Oh. That's your nipple? My bad. Don't mind me"** morning stretch, our first waking moments are usually spent playing *"The Poke Game,"* where we continue to poke around to see if she's game. Never mind the fact that we're not even really that horny half of the time. We're still contractually obligated to at least *try*. Its bylaw 32b in section XVII of the terms and conditions rulebook we all receive with our penises at birth. A man completely disregarding this process every morning (weekends included) for a quick jump in the shower means one of three things:

I. He's married and he needs to get back home without your scent on him.

II. He's gay, and you're his beard.

III. You have a stupid and stale vagina, and the thought of having "extra" sex with you disturbs the shit out of him.

D) Your oral consistently causes a chorus of wincing, "Wait's!!!", and "What are you doing's??" There is a time and a place for hysterectomies and circumcisions, as well as specific tools and equipment, and it's probably not a good idea to ever assume that *right now is the time,* their *bedroom* is the place, and your teeth and dry-ass fingers are the proper tools.

E) You have a zero day return policy. It's a commonly known fact that women of a certain age will do anything to *"keep their numbers down"*—what some 25-40 year old single women do to keep their number of sexual partners at a "respectable" level while still having a somewhat active sex life. This includes the storage of an ex's contact info for a set period of time, kept in case of dire *"I just left a wedding reception. I'm drunk, I'm depressed, and I need some. Right. Now."* no-strings attached (Ha!) emergency.

If you're over 25 and you've never received that phone call from an ex, just be thankful that you obviously have a great personality.

On the flip side, if...

F) After sex with you, men consistently disappear out of thin air like David Blaine...maybe the next time you're at Borders you need to pick up the *"Tantric Tricks"* box set and leave *"The Tipping Point"* on the shelves. Unless they're sociopaths or Kappas, most guys view *"Hey, she wants to continue having sex with me!"* as an incentive to stay around, not pull a disappearing act. If guys you're dating always seem to turn into magicians after you've had sex, maybe they're just not that into your vagina.

G) Your lovemaking lawyering is useless. While it's true that men do occasionally turn down sex, it's also true that our "No's" are usually as weak as Malibu rum and can easily be coerced into an immediate change of heart. There's another section in the aforementioned penis rulebook addressing this.

"Male humans are allowed exactly once thwarting per quarter in response to a female human's sexual advances. Yet, if said female is persistent, one is obligated to reluctantly participate, as not to upset the female sex Goddesses."

If cursed with crippled coochie, though, you're liable to hear *"Nah, babe. I'm good. I need to finish these popsicles before they melt. Maybe later."*

9. The idea of a woman willingly and enthusiastically performing and enjoying fellatio matters more than the actual act. Influenced by countless Eazy-E CDs and discussions in high school, most young men are obsessed with the idea that someone would willingly put their mouths on their penises to provide sexual pleasure, and many of us become consumed with finding someone, *anyone*, who'll perform that feat for us. It doesn't matter

37

that any head any guy has ever received by a woman who was younger than 24 years old has probably been terrible[13]. As long as we were receiving it, we felt like we'd uncovered a secret hidden treasure filled with wet tongues and willing trollops. As you get older, the actual head technique of the women you're with usually gets better, but the euphoria you feel actually lessens, mainly because you began to realize that head itself is kind of a overrated feeling. Sure, it feels great, but it pales in comparison to actual sex.

Still, despite the fact that it can kind of be physically underwhelming, we still relish the idea of a woman we're with being willing to enthusiastically perform it. There's no bigger ego trip, and no better way to take your mind back to the happily nostalgic days of cafeteria food, homecoming dances, and daydreaming in physics class, wondering which cheerleader might help you partake in this elusive penile pleasure.

10. Clubbing while horny is no different than grocery shopping while hungry. In both cases, you'll just end up spending too much for some shit you didn't even really want. That snaggle-toothed stripper you lured back to your apartment after a night of clubbing while in a sexual drought *and* that day you skipped breakfast and lunch, hit the supermarket, and somehow managed to convince yourself you needed 15 Digiorno's pizzas? The exact same thing.

---

[13] The best "head window" for women seems to be when they're somewhere between 24 and 31. This way, they're old enough to actually know what they're doing and not be disgusted by it, and still too young for the *"Damn, I'm doing all of this purposeless dick-sucking for no reason"* realization to start seeping in. Good times for all. –*T.C.*

11. Sex tapes should be left to the experts. But, anyone can be an expert. Although actually watching them "perform" was like watching paint fuck, the careers of Kim Kardashian and Ray J are concrete proof that a sex tape can benefit both parties. Slutty celebrity ambition aside, a properly made video recording of you and your lover's most intimate moments can be a private, visual confirmation of your mutual love and affection, a relevant boon in moments of libido recession, or an audition tape to host BET's *106 and Park*. While I'm assuming most of us haven't actually recorded ourselves, I'm 100% sure everyone has thought about it at least once. With this in mind, take notes.

A) Do make sure you have enough light. Unless you want your video to look and sound like a Triple X version of *The Blair Witch Project*, it's a good idea to make sure your filming area has proper lighting. There are few things more disorientating and disappointing than anticipating great theater but witnessing *Shadow Sex Puppets 3* when you finally play it back. This is also one of the many reasons why you should always keep a spare flare or strobe light in your bedroom closet.

B) Don't show your face. Roughly 92.8% of amateur sex videos are made with cell phone camcorders, which explains how these things seem to leak out so frequently and easily. Because of this, you should probably make sure your face is somewhat obscured. While this can be accomplished with creative positioning, personally, I think twin Zorro masks are the best way to go.

C) Do make sure that all parties involved realize they are being recorded. Although the mini cam you've hidden in that Puma shoebox on your dresser saved you from rape charges last year, it's in everyone's best interest if each participant knows they're being filmed. And, although I can appreciate the comic relief in slipping in a whispered *"Yeah baby, smile for daddy's camera"* between a chorus of unintelligible moans and *"Say my names"*...

D) ...Don't decide to let them know they're being recorded halfway through the act. Unless, of course, you want to get stabbed.

E) Do have a sense of humor. Camcorders have a funny tendency to record the type of stuff you don't see in that flattering mirror you pass 27 times a day or those 9 year old Facebook profile pictures that you've convinced yourself you still actually look like. You'll need a sense of humor if you watch yourself and receive visual confirmation that your *real* nude and sexual self is more Janet Reno than Janet Jacme.

F) Don't allow any unexpected visitors. This includes (but isn't limited to): pets, babies, roaches, pet baby roaches, parents, window voyeurs (unless planned), annoying ringtones, midgets (unless bored), and angry ex-girlfriends (unless banging).

G) Do handle the recording duties by yourself. Even if he allowed you to borrow the camera he uses to watch the barbershop, it's probably not the best idea to ask your barber to record you and your girl, and it's definitely not the best idea to let his janky-ass watch if he *volunteers*.

H) Don't blast your sexin' mixtape so loudly that you can't hear anything else. Call me crazy, but when you replay this video, I'm assuming you're going to want to actually hear each other instead of Trey Songz. You want the neighbors to know your name, not his.

I) Don't be Chris Brown. If you recall, a week or so after Rihanna and Chris Brown were involved in their infamous altercation on the way to the Grammys, nude pictures of Rihanna[14] somehow found their way to the internet, an apparent strike from someone in Chris Brown's camp to fight fire with some fire of their own. Basically, don't be the paragon of bitchassedness who accidently leaks you and your lovers most intimate moments on the internet after a bad break-up or argument. There's no possible excuse or justification for this, unless, of course, you want your own reality show.

12. Everyone who's ever said that they accidentally got pregnant or contracted an STD because a condom broke is fucking lying. Look, I understand why people are reluctant to admit they've been having unprotected sex outside of marriage. Any person with a working brain and a Borders Rewards card should be very aware of the risks associated with condom-less sex, and knowingly partaking in it makes you seem (at best) irresponsible and (at worst) fucking stupid. But, as the thousands of kids throwing tantrums in Wal-Mart everyday proves, many people are giving condoms the middle finger. And, although an "educated" person *should* know better, "knowing better" sometimes just means we know better than to admit we've been volunteering at the AIDS Task

---

[14] Although the Ray J/Kim Kardashian tape was a disappointment you definitely can't say that about the leaked Rihanna nude photos. My Goodness!!! Who knew little Ri-Ri was built like that? Seriously, I hadn't been that pleasantly surprised and shocked since the unexpected Kerry Washington/Dania Ramirez sex scene in *She Hate Me.* –T.C.

Force Saturday mornings and playing the pull-out game Saturday nights.

13. There are actually a ton of things you can do when your neighbors are *doing the do*. If you're reading this book, you're probably at an age where you're most likely in or aren't that far removed from a social or financial situation that somewhat dictates your living options. When this occurs, whether it's a college dormitory or inner-city apartment complex, the proximity of people around you means that you can't help but become a bit more familiar with your neighbors and suitemates than you'd probably like to be. You know that the girl across the hall cooks Ethiopian food every other Friday, that the guy on the first floor with the blue BMW never speaks or makes eye contact, and that the two women living below you receive a strange brown UPS package at least twice a week (and you're convinced that they're building an atomic bomb).

Eventually, you get used to all of this. In fact, for some people these occurrences give their homes more character. But, along with these relatively minor quirks and annoyances comes something so unavoidably personal, obvious, distinct, and spell-bounding that it produces such a smorgasbord of contrasting feelings and emotions you have no idea what the hell to do.

For most, it usually starts the exact same way. You'll be on your laptop in your bedroom, surfing for farmers markets, animal shelters, and places to volunteer, when the first barely audible *"Ooh"* is heard. Since you're sitting near a window, the first thought is to dismiss this as one of the random street sounds (*i.e.: H&M sandals scraping the pavement, the barking of asexual shih tzus and their bisexual owners, etc*) associated with living in a recently gentrified neighborhood.[15] Then, the *Oohs* will slowly crescendo. This, combined with the now sporadic wall thumps and random smacks, creates the unmistakable evidence of next-door nookie. The neighbors are definitely doing the nasty, you'll definitely be their reluctant audience for the next five to one hundred and thirty-five minutes, and there's definitely nothing you can do about it...*or is there?*

A) Listen, laugh, and learn. Accidentally listening to other people having sex is the auditory version of the car wreck. Once you hear it, you know you shouldn't be paying attention, but some uncontrollable force makes it so that you can't help but pay attention. Linkin Park and the entire Wu-Tang Clan could be in your bedroom performing live, but once you hear those sounds, nothing is loud enough and no Zen concentration is good enough for you to block them out. But, realistically, after you get past the initial *"Damn...they're really over there screwing, ain't they?"* shock, what better option is there than to just listen?

Since they had the utter audacity to include you in their Sunday morning sex session, be an *active* audience member. Turn off your television, and shut your window to block out distracting sounds. When this is done, find a

---

[15] In my hometown (Pittsburgh), many of the lower income blacks displaced by gentrification are moving to the suburbs. It's especially interesting watching the dynamics play out in Penn Hills, a suburb east of Pittsburgh which for years was the place for middle class blacks to escape, for lack of a better term, "Niggas". Now, the niggas are coming. But, surprisingly, the high school basketball and football teams are getting progressively worse. Go figure. –*T.C.*

glass and rub peroxide on your wall.[16] Also, what better way is there to really get to *really* know your neighbors than to hear them at their most vulnerable? *("Is he a sadist? Is she a drama queen? Wow. Now I know why they spend so much time with that midget.")* These are the type of things you need to know when deciding who from your building to borrow bleach from or invite to your Super Bowl party.

And, since genuine laughs are tough to come by in a recession, what better and cheaper comic relief is there than hearing your neighbor's boyfriend scream *"Release the hounds"* right before he climaxes?

B) Masturbate. According to a 1997 study by Sexual Education professors at the University of Shadyside, and published in their medical journal, there are three normal adult human responses to the sound of lovemaking: **Disgust, Arousal, and Disgust at your arousal**

Apparently this sound triggers a release of uncontrollable endorphins, an evolutionary trait that enhances our reproductive potential and progress. Basically, whenever we hear that sound, we're urged to **compete** as soon as possible. By my calculations, you'll have at least a 66% chance of being aroused. Since this is true, why not just pop two birds with one bone?

Okay, I completely made that study and the university up, but doesn't it at least sound like it should be true?

---

[16] Not sure if this actually works. I just saw MacGyver do it once and thought it was cool. —*T.C*

C) Up the ante. My personal favorite, ante-upping occurs when the spider-monkeys next door annoy *and* arouse you and your significant other so much that you decide to make it your own personal mission to out-coitus them.

Shit, you already have concrete evidence that the walls in your cheap-ass apartment are thin, so why not have a little *"So you think you can fuck?"* competition?[17] Be a banshee. Smack the wall and your (willing) girlfriend's ass simultaneously. Growl and meow. Use more and more cowbell. Speak in tongues. Invite your pets. Shit, your girlfriend's cat always tries to join in anyway, so let her participate this time. Buy an echo machine, and have it do whatever the hell it is that echo machines actually do. The possibilities are endless.

14. Sometimes "Technical Difficulties" might occur. Whether it's because of stress, fatigue, alcohol, or an especially haunting episode of *Cold Case* on your mind, sometimes shit just doesn't happen. Even if you're a perfectly healthy male with a perfectly working wang, there will be times when your batter just can't muster enough energy to even swing. It's nothing to be ashamed of though, and as long as you give your sure to be disappointed girl a convincing Good Will Hunting ("It's

---

[17] The best ante-upping movie scene of all-time occurs in *Forgetting Sarah Marshall*, when Sarah (Kristen Bell) overhears her ex-boyfriend Peter (Jason Segal) having sex with Rachel (Mila Kunis) in the hotel room next door, and wakes her reluctant boyfriend Aldous (Russell Brand) to "compete" with them. This movie also contains the most awkwardly unfunny full-frontal male nudity seen ever, the best on-screen performance of a song written about a vampire, the most recent entry on my own personal Natalie Portman all-star team (*comprised of small chested white women I'm inexplicably attracted to. Right now, Mila Kunis is manning the backcourt with Emmy Rossum*), and the incomparable Jack McBrayer. Basically, the entire movie is fucking awesome. –*T.C.*

not your fault. It's not your fault.") everything should be cool.

15. "Check your ego at the door" and "Pay attention" are really the only forms of "Better Sex" advice that actually matter. "Checking your ego" means...

A) No sack "cuteness" or porn star posturing. You're not performing, and nobody is watching. Sex is sloppy and messy, and great sex is sloppier and messier than an Ohio chicken farm. If you don't want to get sloppy and messy, *don't have sex*, because your new hairdo will get sweated out and your French manicured toes will get spit at and came on.

B) No holding back. No *"You know what, I'll let him hit today, but he's not getting any head"* or *"Yea, I guess I'll go down there, but only for a quarter of a lick"* or *"I'm only going to cum once. He hasn't earned two O's yet."* As funny as this sounds, there are people who actually do this. Some are probably reading this right now, holding their wack sex having heads in shame. Bastards. Again, if you're going to have sex...*have sex*. There's no shame in not having it, just in intentionally making it wack.

Ladies, the bedroom isn't a place to further your fight for women's equality. I know, I know, I know. Nothing proves the existence of Patriarchy more than the fact that much of the language regularly used to describe sex implies male dominance and female submission (i.e.: "He beat it up," "She gave him some," etc), and this is a wrong that should be righted. But, once you actually get into the bedroom, it's really not that serious. To rephrase, making everything a super serious fight for coitus civil rights will probably dead his *and* your libido.

46

If he turns you around so you can get in the doggy-style position, it's probably not the best idea to say *"Wait a second! Are you trying to call me a bitch? Rosa Parks didn't do doggy for the bus driver, and I won't either!!!"* Plus, I can imagine it being hard to be a rad fem or womanist with cum on your nose.

Also, fellas, some backs aren't immediately breakable. While you may think your penis is a praise-worthy pleasure pole, not all women are going to subscribe to the same belief. Have a plan B. If plan B doesn't work, have a plan C. If plan C doesn't work, paint her toenails, have a RedBull, and write a haiku convincing her to try your plan D.

"Paying attention" means...

A) If you're showing your lover that "genius" head technique you learned while watching *Ghetto Booty 27*, and they're making a face that looks like they're witnessing a horse being circumcised while you do it, maybe it's time to retire that move.

B) That odd *magic zone* coincidence—where your partner gets even more aroused than usual—that seems to occur when you whisper a certain something in her ear or call him a certain name (I'm partial to **"Shaft in Africa,"** just in case y'all were wondering), isn't a coincidence. Whatever you're doing, it's working. Keep doing it. Pay attention, asshole.

16. There are at least 125 Unspoken and Unuttered Sexual Commandments (*each representing sexual rules and ways of living we never actually admit to be true,*

even though they usually are) Here are four of my favorites:

A) If in a sexual drought, thou shalt drive thyself crazy with the assumption that everyone else in the entire world is currently having the best sex anyone's ever had.

B) Thou shalt use masturbation as an efficient way to alleviate boredom, hunger, anxiety, confusion, anger, frustration, headaches, joint pain, excessive happiness, grief, loneliness, righteousness, despair, and self-esteem. Also, when finished, thou shall experience a small moment of euphoria quickly followed by intense self-loathing and regret when cleaning up.

C) Thou shalt not, under any circumstances, ever publicly admit to having period sex.

D) If in a relationship, thou shalt forgo condoms when "acceptable" period of time has passed. In this case, "acceptable period of time" is figured out by using a complex matrix involving some combination of how much time you've spent together, how many people you assume they've been with, a picture of their ex, the number of degrees you both possess, and how recently you've seen Magic Johnson on TV.

17. There are some things about sex that truly fucking suck. Although saying this seems blasphemous, sex isn't all good all of the time. And, aside from the obvious (*Potentially unwanted pregnancies, STDs, etc*) there's some shit about sex that we could all really do without. **This includes:**

A) Post-coital clean-up. With all the talk about the economy and new job creation, why hasn't someone founded a post-coital clean-up company yet? Seriously, as annoying as it can be to clean up after sex, who *wouldn't* pay someone to come in your crib and take care of all the wet spots, used condoms, dead midgets, and dirty sheets for you while you were still in your uber-lazy post sex coma?

B) Hearing people much younger or much older than you talk about it. The world would be a much better place if we could go through the rest of our lives never hearing anyone more than ten years younger (*because you're always tempted to just tell them to shut the fuck up*) or fifteen years older (*because you're always tempted to just tell them that nobody wants to think about your old ass fucking*) than us refer to anything sexual in any context ever again.

C) The "*I didn't do a complete and thorough clean-up of my man parts after sex last night, and now it's the morning and my wang is practically super-glued to my boxers*" face. By the way, this face is the first cousin of the "*I didn't do a complete and thorough clean-up of my man parts after sex last night, and now its the morning and I have to pee and my hole is glued tighter than Sam Jackson's wig in* Pulp Fiction" face

18. The more I learn, the more I realize I still don't really know shit. When younger, your limited world view and relative lack of experience places a ceiling on your sexual and relationship wisdom. You think you know everything because you have no idea that there's still an entire stadium-sized room for sexual, mental, and emotional growth. As you get older and more

49

experienced, the cocksure naivety begins to subside, with a more reasoned and rational approach to sexuality taking its place.

Basically, it's like Tarzan first discovering that while he may have been the King of his own Jungle, an entire new and humbling world with scary female orgasm beasts[18] exists outside of it, and his survival depends on his ability to adapt and adjust.

You can't expect to bag and bed bad tiger chicks with caveman game.

---

[18] You have to admit that the vagina is one of the most intimidating substances on the planet. Imagine if you had never seen one before, and the Earth was invaded by a bunch of 8 foot tall vagina monsters. You're telling me that a bunch of drippy, stretchy, flappy, leaky, multi-colored beings that spit random red substances at their whim wouldn't scare the shit out of you?? –T.C.

Rate at Your Own Risk
Why Men Should Never, Ever, Ever, Ever Tell a Woman Her "Score" (Even If She Asks)

By Panama Jackson

There are bad ideas in life, and then there are *bad* ideas. Terrible ideas. Ideas worse than *"Hey, stay here while I go in the woods by myself to see exactly why none of our friends seem to be returning my text messages"* while you're camping at Crystal Lake. Sharing your rating scale with any close women friends is definitely one of these horrendous ideas. Here's why you should file it in with "Pulling a Plaxico"—*getting shot...by your own hand...with your own gun...in the thigh...at a nightclub...in New York State*—on the list of *"Things you should avoid at all costs."*

1. Your "rating" will never be good enough. Unless you call her a dime[19]—*for those unfamiliar with upwardly mobile urban dialect, dime = 10 cents = perfect 10*—the rating will have to be explained. If you call her a 7, why isn't she an 8? If you call her an 8, why isn't she a 10...and who exactly would qualify? You see, you're going to have to explain exactly what keeps her from the highest possible ranking in a way that also stops her from being pissed. Basically, you're going to have to lie.

---

[19] Very rarely do we actually do a full-scale analysis to come up with the ranking. We see a woman, and then say, "she's an 8." Somebody might disagree and maybe a short discussion on her "merits" will ensue, but very rarely is it a long discussion. It's kind of a quick overall gut assessment with no scientific data. Basically, it's exactly like we're in the Tea Party. –P.J.

51

Even though she said, "*I won't be mad...*" she's lying. Throw something at her.

2. If you call her a dime, you give her carte blanche to be a dick.[20] The fucked up side to letting a woman know you think she's a dime is that you'll probably also have to explain exactly why she qualifies. Basically, you're about to give her a psyche blow job because she will want to know everything you like about her. Further, she will tell you things she isn't happy with (i.e. "*You know, I've always thought my boobs were a bit too juicy and perky*"), and you'll probably respond with a variant of "Girl, are you crazy..." and proceed to tell her why she's so hot; all the while not realizing that you're basically telling this woman you'd sell your left testicle for the chance to see her naked.

Now, it becomes a problem because she has a leg up on your ass. Let's say she's interested in you. And, more than likely, if she's a dime, you're interested in her. She now knows you think she's the most perfect shit on Earth. You've put it all out there, laying out your

---

[20] While many men seem to believe that trying to date a supermodel is a must-do, I'm here to tell you it's probably an overrated experience. Why? Well...

1. Nobody will give a shit about you. Look at Jermaine Dupri. That smurf has GRAMMYS and millions, but all anybody could talk about for years was the fact that he somehow, someway snagged Janet Jackson.
2. Paranoia. All Black men come with a certain level of paranoia. Add a fine woman to the mix and all of a sudden he becomes a jealous imbecile suspecting even midgets of having a chance of stealing his woman.
3. You can't do any better. Anybody else you date will probably be a step down, looks-wise, and since men are shallow by nature, it's going to matter a bit more than it actually should. What this means is that you can't fuck it up or you'll have to hear for the rest of your life how you blew it with the hot chick. And, you know what? Because you're shallow, you'll actually care. Date 6's. –*P.J.*

feelings for her and basically relinquishing any possible *"I'm too cool to really care about you that much"* pretense we love to use when first meeting a woman.

And, don't get it twisted. Yeah, you told her how fine she is, but you also stroked her ego and made sure that she knew that there was at least somebody out there who appreciated her in all of her splendor. Now, you had better hope that she ain't no triflin' heffa who will decide to use the fact that she knows you're interested against you. Yeah, she might like you too, but we know that some women play games like this. Bottom line, throw something at her.

3. The women will now probably run to their other friends and tell them what you rated them, thus causing other women to come to you asking for ratings, thus causing all kinds of unnecessary ruckus amongst a group of friends. Women are some jealous-ass creatures. Men are as well, I'm aware. Shit, I'm jealous you read all of The Champ's chapters before reading this. But, women love big-leaguing each other. And, maybe it isn't blatant or direct, but you can see the glazed over look in most women's eyes when they know they have something on another woman, like a cheetah spotting a busted-ass gazelle limping through the grass. No words have to be spoken. The worst thing you can do to the dynamics of a group of women you're cool with is validate that there's a definite pecking order.

4. Ultimately, you just might fuck up your chance to see her naked. If you go running your trap about what you think about her and it's not good enough (#1), you might just fuck up your shot because she'll go to doing that woman-thinking and assume that since you don't think she's perfect, you're not into her like she hoped. Her feelings are hurt, you have to do damage control, and she's done with you.

Of course, this assumes she likes your dumb ass anyway. Bottom line?

Man Law #1: Keep your mouth shut, homey.

21ˢᵗ Century Chivalry

By The Champ

For many of us, the concept of chivalry died years ago, neglected so long that it ended up gaunt and emaciated, starving to death outside of a KFC because no one could spare him the big piece of chicken. Well, The Champ is here to say that we're wrong. Chivalry isn't dead or even dying...just in need of a bit of a makeover. An update. A reboot. A few minor tweaks and adjustments for the 21st century, and an explanation for why it's so necessary.

1. Men *still* should always pay for (at least) the first three dates. It doesn't matter if the guy is a grad student working at Starbucks dating a CPA making 80k a year. If they're dating, the man should always cover at least the first three dates. This may seem a bit antiquated, but this universal rule actually benefits both parties. If she's really into him, she won't mind the fact that the first couple of dates have been at Borders, the cheese dog stand at the Arts Festival, and the sample soup counter at Costco. If she's feeling him, but does mind the limited spending dates, that's all the proof he needs that she's probably not the woman for him. See how easy that works?

If things are going well, by date four she can offer to at least provide the setting (and maybe even pay), and the man should consider accepting her offer. Also, I've always thought that if a woman invites a man over for dinner, she should be obligated to have sex with him if she can't cook. While this may seem somewhat unfair, it's even more unfair to send a guy home with *Salmonella* poisoning *and* an unopened pack of Trojans.

2. If you're a man and a woman, any woman, is within 15-20 feet of you and approaching the same door you are, you must *always* **attempt to open it and let her walk through first, even if you're coming from an awkward angle. If the woman is within 20-40 feet and walking at a pace which insures that she'll be at the same door you're about to enter within 5-7 seconds, you can walk through the door first, but you must hold the door for her.** This is pretty non-negotiable. If you're a man and you don't open doors for women, and don't wait as a human doorstop for a woman that's less than ten seconds away from the door, you're probably a **Diva Dude.** (More on Diva Dudes later, I promise.)

Sure, there are extenuating circumstances (i.e.: *you have crutches, you really, really have to pee, she's running from the cops, etc*) but this is another one of the rules that will never change.

Plus, as an added bonus, there's no better way of getting a really good and clear booty peek. Women always seem to jiggle the hips a little extra whenever a door is being held open for them. I think it's a primitive mating mechanism actually, some evolutionary correlation between held doors, jiggled hips, and ovaries, but I really have no idea.

In the rare case that you happen to come across some woman who feels as if any male holding a door for her is a symptom of 2000 years of Western oppression and male privilege, **do** shrug your shoulders and *continue to hold the door*. And, even though you might be tempted, **don't** pat her on the head when she walks by.

There's really only one instance where you probably shouldn't open the door for a woman, and that's when she's with another man who looks as if it might be *her* man. Door opening now is a no-no because it basically shows the other man up, visibly usurping one of his most important roles. You don't want to cause some poor stranger any unnecessary anguish. He doesn't need to hear *"What, some stranger can open the door for me and your lazy ass can't??? Maybe I should have give HIM the shower quickie this morning instead of you!!!"* when he gets home. Remember; happy woman means happy man, and happy men means **less crime.**

3. Men should always volunteer to sleep in the "wet spot." Why? Because making her the one who always has to lay down to sleep in the spot on the bed where you just finished having sex is a sure-fire way to ensure that her spot won't be too wet for too much longer. Remember, wet spots can also be very *cold,* and *coldness anywhere on the skin at night* is such a female libido killer that it might as well just be called *man without any status or potential.* Along with *"walk on the side closest to the curb, even though if a car does actually jump the curb, it's probably going to kill you both anyway,"* this is one of those you just have to take for the team.

4. When speaking to a stranger or a woman you're interested in, never voluntarily bring up any of the following topics: the size of your salary, bank account, or penis; how many women you've slept with; how many women you plan to sleep with; your plans to sleep with her; your blog; your usual standard of physical attractiveness in a mate, and what a woman would need to do in order for him to compromise; anything regarding

her ass, hips, dick-sucking lips, or chest; your mom; her dad[21].

5. Always let women within 10 feet of you go first (and leave first) in elevators, buses, cabs, and any other object that moves and also has doors. This one is a bit tricky actually because of what sometimes happens when a man who is closer to a bus door than a woman is hesitates for a second—a sign letting the woman know she can go on first. The woman, used to years of emaciated chivalry, isn't expecting this, so she isn't even paying attention. They both end up just standing there for a moment, motionless, and sometimes that one second pause is all the justification an asshole bus or cab driver needs to close the door and speed off. Now, if the woman is more than 10 feet away, then yeah, it's probably best that you just get on. Waiting then just becomes some awkward, urban, rope-less double-dutch game with you waiting to jump in, never a good look.

This is also a great time to watch women's behinds. Seriously, if a man's ever in doubt about how to smoothly navigate any situation involving women and doors, if he just positions himself in a way that allows for the best ass peak possible, he'll probably be right. You see, there are ways to appreciate women's figures without doing the piss-boy pirouette, and chivalry actually allows for many of them. Nothing beats watching a nice pair of hips walk up a few city bus stairs. I'm actually beginning

---

[21] You know, it's actually really tragic that "daddy issues" is more of a jokey scarlet letter we attach to needy and insane broads than something we really discuss. Really, if the women are all insane, and the men are all going to kill at least 1/10 of a person a piece, who knows where our community is heading? *–P.J.*

to think that chivalry is just a convoluted system devised for men to look at as much ass as possible. Underneath all of those layers of clothing and armor, those damn knights and maidens must have been a bunch of freaks.

6. If on a crowded bus or train, you must give up your seat to elderly men and *most* women, on one condition...*there are no reasonably available seats in front of you.* Now, by *reasonably available* I mean, of course the vacant seat with the booger or next to the naked crackhead doesn't count, but you're not obligated to get up if there are a couple clean seats in front of you. If not, don't even make a big deal out of it, just stand and head to the back. I've even begun doing the pre-emptive stand, where you don't even bother to sit down if a seat is available on a crowded bus because you know you'll be giving it up soon anyway.

7. The man should always be the first one to change his status to *"In a relationship"* on Facebook or any other social networking websites.[22] You see, a woman's friends probably pay more attention to that stuff than a typical

---

[22] More Facebook chivalry.

1. If a man and a woman have just began dating, but aren't Facebook friends, the man should initiate the add request process. Subsequently, if a man doesn't initiate the add request process (or if the man initiates and woman declines), it's perfectly okay to think that they're hiding something (Most likely? They are probably hiding you) or they're just not that into you.
2. If in a relationship, if a man decides to befriend a few of his girlfriend's friends, he should befriend all of them...not just the cute ones
3. Actually, disregard number 2. He'd be more safe just friending the ones who are less attractive than his girlfriend. If one of her hotter friends makes a request to be your friend, either ignore her, or make sure you name drop your girlfriends name in any correspondence you all have. Who knows, it could be a trap. –T.C.

man's friends are going to, which means they're much more likely to give her hell for changing her status before you changed yours than your friends would. Plus, when a woman does that first, it usually screams *"My name is Ation. Desper Ation."* and you don't want to put her in that position. Subsequently, unless it was a particularly foul *"she cheated on me with my nephew"* type of break-up, the man should probably also wait until his ex has changed her status back to single before he does.

8. A man can never say "please" and "thank you" too much, except in the bedroom, where they should be given the condiment treatment: Best used with light sprinkles. The bedroom in itself is a paradox where the common rules of chivalry don't exist. For instance, saying "please" during a sexual act is a bit tricky because "please" accompanies a request. Depending on his disposition, body language, and penis size, "please" could be interpreted as *"a playful request lightening the mood,"* *"a considerate lover,"* or *"an annoyingly desperate dude who should just shut the fuck up and be happy that his cornball ass is getting some."* There's basically no in-between, no gray area with this, exactly why he needs to be absolutely sure about the nature of their sexual relationship before he continues with the *pleases*. Usually in these situations, a slight nudge or eye contact is all that's needed to get his point across, whatever it happens to be. Also, the appropriateness of thank you is just as dependant on the situation. For instance:

After finishing a very fulfilling tryst with your lover, you kiss her, lay flat on your back, and say "thanks baby" while you're still laying there, catching your breath, enjoying that post-sex hazy silence, and reflecting about the entire experience.

In this case, the thank you enhanced the level of intimacy. It's a sweet gesture; two lovers letting each other know that the act which just occurred was greatly valued and appreciated, a stark contrast from...

Right after finishing a fulfilling tryst with a lover, you remove yourself from inside of her, jump out the bed, say "thanks babe" and hop in the shower before she's even moved a muscle.

In this case, the thank you completely disengages the situation of all intimacy, treating the act as if it should be accompanied by a credit card swipe and receipt coming out of her ass like she's a dancer in Nelly's "Tip Drill" video. I understand that all sex isn't going to be love-making, but it still is sex. It's not like she just ironed a shirt for you and made you a grilled-cheese sandwich.

9. Unless she insists on it, a man should always be the first to "Bless." Because of the negative stigma surrounding women (black women especially) and fellatio, its understandable (but still a bit odd) if she doesn't immediately feel comfortable giving head. With that in mind, a 21ˢᵗ century chivalry-minded man shouldn't be the Diva Dude who holds out on his chick because he's playing a game of cunnilingus chicken.

10. Don't bullshit the chivalry Gods. Men, don't break your neck to open doors for every Zoe Saldana you see but refuse to give up your seat for the slightly homely chick with the eclectic teeth. On the same token, women should always acknowledge a chivalrous act. It could be a smile or a thank you or a slight head nod or head or an "accidental" cleavage peak; anything as long as it lets the guy know that his efforts haven't been in vain. If you see a guy doing the doorstop thing for you, the very least you can do is make an effort to sped up your walk so it doesn't seem like he's standing there waiting for the seasons to change in the time it takes your inconsiderate ass to get to the door.

There you go young grasshoppers. Go on now and make The Champ proud.

The Goggles...
...And Why You Should Take Them Off As Soon As Possible If You Ever Catch Yourselves Wearing a Pair

By The Champ

We've all been there before. Regardless of the reasoning behind it, every single person reading this has been in a situation where an outside circumstance made a particular person much more attractive than they usually would have been. It's usually not our fault, though. Sensing that we need some sort of urging to reach our reproductive potential, our brains and our eyes collaborate to play a trick on us; deceiving us into thinking that the beast at the bar is Beyonce and the neighbor we've never really been all that attracted to is all of a sudden an Adonis.

Coined **The Goggles**, these agents of illusion conspire to use our need for coitus against us, and equipping yourself with knowledge of the characteristics of each of the most lecherous forms of **The Goggles** is the only possible defense against them.

WORK GOGGLES—describe what happens when you're in an office environment, and you start making arguments in your head for people you aren't really that attracted to.

"You know, when she sits near the door during Wednesday staff meetings, sometimes her eyes look sexy and mysterious and her breasts look pretty ripe. She also borrowed my stapler last week. Damn flirt. I should probably try to have sex with her."

63

Also, if the new person—someone who's recently been hired—has even a shred of attractiveness, they'll automatically become that office's version of Idris Elba or Rihanna for at least two months without fail. It's just like 7th grade, when the new girl from Texas transferred in and everybody broke their necks to see who'd get her phone number first. And, as soon as the first number was handed out, she was basically forgotten forever. If you hated junior high, you'll probably hate working in an office.

Work Goggles Plusses: Three words—*copy room quickies.* Also, there is the possibility that the constant close contact has allowed you to notice an attractive part of their personality that you may have overlooked in a different setting. And, you know, at least you know that the person has a job. It is a recession and shit.

Work Goggles Minuses: Five words—*don't shit where you eat.* If it (the relationship) does work, you then run the possibility of breaking up just because you're tired of seeing them 24 hours a day every day. If you have sex and the relationship doesn't work, you then create the possibility of your office turning into the West Bank or Newark, New Jersey. There is no greater hell than having to spend 40 hours a week in a workplace divided by someone's sexual activity or relationship status, and rest assured, your co-workers will eventually hate both of you.

Verdict: Unless you're convinced they're your Neo—the one person you're destined to spend the rest of your life with—try to shy away from this.[23] Nine times out of 10, you'll be in your cubicle some time in the near future, reading some horrific "*Do I need to check my microwave for dead kittens?*" type email from that redbone temp you dated two months ago while shaking your head and asking yourself, "*Damn. What the hell was I thinking?????*"

COLLEGE GOGGLES—occur when you're out of school, but you either work near a university or have college students working for or with you. This prolonged contact, along with the viewing of countless Maxim Magazines, WorldStarHipHop.com videos, and Girls Gone Wild infomercials, causes you to assume that most college-aged women are easier than a G.E.D. test for dyslexic kittens.

College Goggles Plusses: Remember this "*...causes you to assume that most college-aged women are easier than a G.E.D. test for dyslexic kittens*"? Well, nowadays, that's probably true. Plus, since most college-aged people are broke and living off of cafeteria food and Ramen noodles,

---

[23] If your horny ass just can't help yourself, here are a few ways to ensure your workplace romance doesn't end up going postal.

1. Shut your trap. Like most criminals, things generally go wrong once one party starts yapping. The optimal situation is for both parties to hush-the-fudge up. The quieter it's kept the more fun the two of you can have.
2. No unnecessary flirtatiousness with the office help. Since you met them at work, they might be a little more attentive to see if you're just a workplace pimp out there trying to give everybody "raises." Even if you don't want them for anything more than just a couple futon workouts, the least you can do is not obviously dismiss them by showing interest in the chick who gives you staples. Keep your supplies to yourself, Mister!
3. Avoid them at all costs. Generally you shouldn't be schlumping anybody who constantly works within 10 feet of you all day. That's just bad mojo. The cutesy stuff like sending mango-scented paper planes and hoping nobody sees it will only last for a good week. After a while, seeing them every minute of the day will get older than John McCain. –*P.J*

65

a date to the food court at the mall is their version of Ruth's Chris Steak House, and will basically guarantee sex.

College Goggles Minuses: If you're over 30, it's generally not a good idea to date people who aren't old enough to legally drink. You never want to have to perform **old man duties**—driving them places, buying beer for their roommates, exposing them to "old-school" rap from 2001, etc—and having sex in a dorm room when you're not college-aged is basically a sign of a complete loser.

Verdict: Since you're basically guaranteed easy, guilt-free sex, this isn't a completely bad thing, especially if you could somehow rationalize to yourself and your God why the hell your 34 year old ass is having sex in the bottom bunk of some 6 × 8 foot dorm room after slithering past the R.A. If you're okay with all of that, knock yourself out, Lil Champ.[24]

DROUGHT GOGGLES—occur when you're going through a longer than usual (and "usual" in this case is relative—for some it could be two weeks; for others, two years) period of a lack of opposite sex contact. This decreases your usual standards tremendously, but at this point, you could really care less. The mailman, your kid's school-bus driver, your parole officer, Karl "The Mailman" Malone, your ex, DMX ...right now, it doesn't matter. You just need to get it done, quickly.

---

[24] Since I'm aware that the thought of sleeping with a college-aged man disgusts most 21 to 95 year old women, I wouldn't be surprised or saddened if I learned that most women reading this completely ignored this part of the chapter. – *T.C.*

Drought Goggles Plusses: There's a chance that you'll feel 100 times better after you break your seal. Once you break that seal, there's a chance you'll be happier, more efficient at work, nicer to pets, more prone to recycle and less prone to commit violent crimes.

Drought Goggles Minuses: There's a chance that you'll feel 100 times worse after you break your seal because you compromised your integrity for something that wasn't really all that good or seal-break worthy anyway.

Verdict: If you ever find yourself with these on, take them off as soon as possible (Read: *Buy a cat. If that doesn't work, masturbate frequently, furiously, and vigorously*). Remember, even a brussel sprout milkshake would taste great if you were hungry enough.

BEER GOGGLES—describes the phenomenon that occurs when you're drunk and horny and every bar room scalawag's attractiveness goes up exponentially in direct correlation with the amount of time left before the bar or club closes, and the amount of "success" you had that night. In equation form:

V (*number of drinks you've had that night*)

Divided by

X (*number of hours left before the bar closes*) ***** **Y** (*number of phone number's you've received that night*) **+1**

Equals

Z (*the thickness of the goggles*)

Going by this formula, if you've had 5 drinks, and there was 1 hour left before closing, and you had only received 1 phone number so far that night, your goggles thickness[25] would be 2.5; a high level, but still a bit under the dangerous 4. People at 4 and above are at the point to where they'll approach and go home with people who they probably wouldn't even sit next to on a bus if they were sober. This is where people hump and give lap dances to empty barstools. Note the scale below:

Goggles Thickness (GT) 1 to 2.5: You'll be interested in (*and possibly even sleep with*) a person you usually wouldn't under most circumstances. Not a terrible choice, but not your first choice either. And, although you won't regret in the morning, you'll probably regret it two weeks later when you go to church and realize your one night stand is the guest pastor that week.

GT 2.5 to 3.5: Not only have you passed the "*I'll regret it in the morning, but I won't care*" mark, the guy you're twerking for in middle of the dance floor is so undesirable that your friends are actively making fun of both of you. Also, even though you won't remember anything, your friends will never let you forget this night.

GT 3.5 to 5: At this point, you start saying things to yourself like, "*I guess she could be a woman.*"

---

[25] If you're single and out drinking on New Years Eve, Halloween, or Valentine's Day, just assume that your goggles thickness level will be at least a 7. – *T.C.*

GT 5 to 6.5: At this point, you start saying things to yourself like, "*I guess it could be a human.*"

Beer Goggles Plusses: Other than the possibility of easy sex with a possible vagrant...none. Unless, of course, you love being the butt of jokes and making frequent trips to the free clinic.

Beer Goggles Minuses: Pretty much every worst-case sexual scenario you can imagine becomes a possibility.

Verdict: Basically, if you're been caught wearing these repeatedly, you need to either stop drinking or only frequent clubs with good looking people.

INTERNET GOGGLES—occur when you've been corresponding through blogs, email, chat, or Instant Messenger with someone you've never met in person. Sometimes these conversations can last hours into the night, creating this tired haze, which gives you unusual stamina as well as unusual freedom with the tongue and spirit.

The tiredness, combined with the lateness and the fact that you're probably wearing your bed clothes, gives the conversation a certain erotic nature, which sometimes leads to caught feelings, phone sex, and, in extreme cases, proclamations of true love and (no lie) marriage proposals.

Internet Goggles Plusses: There's a chance that these are real feelings and not the product of goggles and Google induced tired proclamation and/or act. You could be kindred spirits, soul mates separated by a monitor and hundreds of miles, but...

Internet Goggles Minuses: ...more than likely, you just need to take your horny ass to bed. Being tired can be as much as an intoxicant as Jack Daniels, and being up late vibing with a like-minded member of the opposite sex can be as much as an aphrodisiac as eryngoes or Halle Berry. Plus, you don't want to run the risk of saying or doing something inappropriate and basically ruining a decent friendship.

Verdict: Again, being tired can be just as bad as being drunk. And, again, if you feel like the goggles are getting pretty thick, it's probably time to take your ass to bed. If these feelings and inclinations are real, they'll be just as real at 2pm the next day. Plus, phone sex is just that...*phone sex*. There's no worse feeling than doing the post-coitus clean-up by yourself while subsequently hoping that the person on the other end isn't streaming all of this live on YouTube.

Catching the Running Man
5 Common Things Men Say That Are *Always* Just Us "Running Game"

By The Champ

Although many associate the phrase **running game** with deception and subterfuge, game is nothing but seduction, and men do it to convince the one being "gamed" to do something the gamer wants them to do. It's actually more advertising than artifice, and while it's usually used in a dating or relationship context, you don't have to be a "pimp" or "playa"[26] to practice or appreciate it.

It's a Mercedes commercial that makes you fantasize about how it would feel to drive up to your high school reunion in a new Benz coupe. It's what every career counselor worth their salt would advise you to put on your resumes and cover letters to ensure your prospective employers see you in the most positive light possible. It's all the flattering pictures on your Facebook page you've

---

[26] Four Signs You're Probably Faking the Funk as a "Pretend Playa"

1. You might have access to multiple women (or men) but they're all in the 4 to 6 range in looks. Even if you slept with every homely homeless chick in the country, you're not a playa, just a guy with an unfortunate Facebook page. And lice.
2. You pay for everything. Women who have the game down get their rent paid. Men get clothes and prescription drugs (the health game is mad depressing right now). If you still pay all of your own bills, you're not a playa, you're just a citizen who dates.
3. Nobody actually pursues you. This one seems pretty obvious, but you'd be amazed at how many "playas" aren't in demand. Or, as my good friend Ray Cash would say, are merely pimps in their own fucking mind.
4. You spend every night at a different woman's (or man's) house. You're definitely not a playa, dog. You're just homeless. –*P.J*

deemed taggable, lest one of your friends see what you actually look like.

To be completely frank, the best answer to *"How can I tell if I'm being gamed?"* is *"Are you alive?"* but that would make this chapter much less fun. Instead, I'll just leave you with 5 common things men say that are *never* NOT game.

1. *"I'm not ready for a relationship right now."*

Why it's always game: If you polled every woman who's ever heard this statement from a man, I'd bet at least 90% of them would say they heard it during a variant of the following scenario.

Boy approaches Girl while at National Gout Foundation fundraiser after-party. Girl is visibly enthralled with the neatness of Boy's full beard, Boy's Escada Sentiment, and Boy's proper use of the term "heteronormative" in a sentence. Boy and Girl exchange numbers, and Boy takes Girl on the best two dates of her life. Three weeks later, Girl invites Boy over for "dinner." After dinner, Boy and Girl sit on living room couch and talk. Boy gives Girl best back massage she's ever had. When massage is over, Girl engages Boy in conversation, even though she can hardly concentrate because her vagina is throbbing to the point that she can feel her heart beating down there. Between slips of Sutter Home, Boy nonchalantly mentions that he doesn't want Girl to get the wrong idea because he's "not really ready for a serious relationship."

It's game because, well, we're not idiots. We know exactly what we're doing, exactly how horny she is, and exactly what her expectations were entering the night. We even know that she uncharacteristically decided to wear a matching bra and panties that night. But, because she's already *thisclose* to **go**, saying "*I'm not ready for a commitment*" at that precise moment allows a guy to do commitment-type stuff (read: sex) while always having an "*Hey, I told you I wasn't ready for a serious relationship*" out whenever she presses him for an actual commitment.

Thing is, while the game in this instance was deceiving, it actually is the truth. Although his actions might suggest otherwise, he was telling the truth when he said he's not ready for a relationship. More specifically, he's not ready for a relationship with *her*, but will continue to do relationship stuff until he finds someone he's more *ready for a relationship* for.

2. "You're nobody to me."

Why it's always game: Although most men won't actually come out and tell a woman he's interested in that he thinks she doesn't matter, "*You're nobody to me*" game occurs when a guy treats a beautiful woman as persona non-grata for absolutely no reason. If he sees her with a group of her girlfriends, he'll speak to and hug each of them except her. She tells a joke, he mimics a cricket. And, not only does he pretend to not know her name ahead of time,[27] after she tells him he doesn't even

---

[27] Most beautiful women seem to assume that men already know their names before they've been formally introduced. While this may seem a bit haughty, my theory is that their assumptions are usually correct. Most of us will do everything possible to find out the name, age, occupation, place of residence, shoe size, social security number, favorite movie, favorite color,

remember it the next time they see each other. When it concerns her, he's basically the guy in the audience at a comedy club who's bored and silent while everyone around him is cracking up. And, as most stand-up comics will tell you, if you happen to notice the bored guy, you become obsessed with him. Why isn't he laughing? Is my timing off? Was that joke stale? Did I offend him?

This is game because, well, savvy men know that attractive women are used to men paying attention to them. And, even though they might be attracted to that woman, they also know that ignoring her can reverse the seduction script. Now, *she's paying attention to him*. Why doesn't he talk to me? Should I introduce myself? Why didn't he laugh at my joke? When is he going to approve my friend request? How is it possible that I know his name and he can't even recall mine? Would fellatio help him remember?

By the way, men only do this type of game with women who are used to being showered with male attention. If you don't fall under this category and think a guy is doing the "*You're nobody to me*" dance with you, you're probably dancing by yourself.

3. "You can be intimidating."

Why it's always game: While it's true that a very small percentage of women are intimidating to a very small percentage of men, it's game because well, men don't talk to women who intimidate them. Why? They're intimidated. Duh! If a man actually tells a woman he's

---

and favorite member of Menudo of an extremely attractive woman once we see her for the first time. – *T.C.*

interested that she intimidates him, he must be talking to her. And, if he's actually putting the effort into talking to her, he's not intimidated by her. He's just saying what he think needs to be said to get her to let her guard down, to get her to *prove* to him that she's not intimidating at all.

Also, if she replies, *"What's so intimidating about me?"* she's now given him carte blanche to run off a list of each of her perceived faults *right in front of her face*, basically telling him, *"Hey, I'm not even sure if I'm interested in you yet, but go right ahead and tell me everything you think is fucked up about me. Also, if you say that I'm 'frigid and stiff', I'll make sure to show you exactly how loose I can be in the back of your Chevy Tahoe later tonight."*

4. *"A woman like you is out of my league."*

Why it's always game: A close cousin of *"You can be intimidating"* game, *"A woman like you is out of my league"* manages to combine the reverse bagging paradox dynamic of the *"You can be intimidating"* game with a direct punch to the guilt trip muscle every attractive single woman develops after her 28th . birthday. Basically, (from an aesthetic standpoint) she *is out of his league,* but because of her numerous failed relationships with guys *in her league,* this statement starts an avalanche of re-evaluatory mental guilt caused by the memories of all the mundane dudes she's overlooked. His faux self-deprecation becomes an intoxicant, putting her under a spell of *hownormalcanimakemyselfseem* just so he'll give *her* a chance.

5. *"I don't know. I'll try to fit you in, but I'm just really busy with a few projects right now."*

Why it's always game: Ah, yes; the *"super busy man"* game. He's super focused, man. This week alone he has eight projects due, he's studying for the LSAT, teaching a bartending class, attending a Bar Mitzvah, performing an exorcism, and releasing a line of urban professional lounge wear for midgets and new parolees. He's getting his grind on, and he wishes he could make more time for her; but for now, the Wendy's drive thru and those 15 minutes in his parking lot will do. And, she's okay with this because he's a busy man, and it makes her feel even better that this important man is making any time in his busy schedule for her.

It's game because no man on Earth has ever been that busy. Shit, even God had time to hit the strip club the night after he created Kenya Moore. But, the *super busy man* knows nothing dries panties quicker than the thought of a needy man, so he gives the impression that he's the complete antithesis. He could be free the entire weekend, but a well-timed *"90 minutes just freed up for me Friday night. You down?"* text to six different women he's already played the super busy card with will have them biting like bucktoothed piranhas.

I guess this chapter is all the proof a woman needs that men are double-talking, selfish, and inconsiderate assholes. But, an entire lifetime spent trying to navigate *woman game (What? You don't think your 3-inch heels or intentionally playing "hard to get" qualifies as game as well?)* has left me with just one thing to say in response to that: **It takes one to know one.**

Going Green
A Very Smart Rant from The Champ

Personally, I've always felt that women should rule the world.

Wait, let me rephrase that. Women actually do rule the world already. How else can you explain how and why dozens of Thai restaurants are popping up in every city along the eastern seaboard? I mean, other than Bobby Flay and people actually from Thailand, nobody eats Thai food except for women. But, they're tearing down steakhouses and strip clubs left and right to put up places with names like "The Smiling Banana Leaf" and "The Burning Anus." If you think I'm playing, peak your head in any urban Thai restaurant and you'll see nothing but groups of single women humming to Beyonce's "Single Ladies" while dancing in their chairs and eating chicken satay. And, every once in a while, you might see a dominant woman ordering dishes for her emasculated and petrified boyfriend, while using all of her *"Why should I consider anal if you never try new things for me?"* woman guilt points to strong-arm him into eating.

Anyway, while women do definitely rule the world, they're missing a genius public relations specialist to remind everyone of this fact *and* help them take full advantage of it. Think about it. Imagine if women had a Karl Rove or even Diddy-like hype man at their disposal. The world as we know it would be a universe of woman omnipotence and dominion, where all the world's men would be coerced to attend *Testosterone Nullification* camps to cement our status as sex slaves, and where all industry, time-travel, and farming equipment were mercilessly controlled by the fairer gender.

Okay, maybe this just shows that I've been watching a bit too much Cinemax After Dark[28], but the point remains: **There are many, many things I envy about the opposite sex.** But, for the sake of time (and this book's total word count) I'll just name four.

1. There are more of them where it counts. Although we outnumber them on Earth, women out populate men in every country that fucking matters. Seriously, look it up! From the United States of America to any country worth traveling to in Europe, South America, Asia, or Africa, there's more of them then us in pretty much every preferred travel destination, and basically any country with a GNP larger than Harvard's endowment. They also outnumber us in any populous situation that anyone gives a damn about (i.e.: college campuses, popular and safe night time bar and clubbing options, entertaining television ensembles, etc), facts that *should* easily lead to their world domination and an easy justification for more threesomes, but they just seem content with using their numbers to dominate talk show live audiences.

2. They live long as hell. This is an admirable trait, although I'd probably live for 95 years also if I could use all the money I saved from never having to pay for

---

[28] **Extremely Naked (and extremely offensive) Dating Truth #23:** Both **men** and **women** (occasionally) fantasize about the types of lesbians that don't really exist in real life. In this sense, Cinemax After Dark is the grown-up's Santa Claus, and Rosie O'Donnell is the day you realized Santa's just a fat fuck at the mall with a third-hand grizzly bear suit and a rock hard pint of Tanqueray in his pocket (at least, you *hope* that's a rock hard pint of Tanqueray in his pocket)—*T.C.*

drinks, dates, or club admission fees towards better health care.

3. They have a much, much, much, much greater tolerance for pain.[29] Forget about their capacity to endure pregnancy, childbirth, periods, broken hymens, and the existence of Sarah Palin, and just let me tell you these two quick stories.

Several years ago, I dated a woman who'd get Brazilian waxed on a regular basis, an extremely sadistic process which is basically the male equivalent of allowing a rabid Persian cat to claw out your pubic hairs after accidentally spilling pancake syrup and bleach on your lap. On mild days she'd run a couple laps around the Highland Park reservoir in Pittsburgh immediately after her appointments.

One morning a couple summers ago, I accidentally stuck my pinkie with a thumbtack. Figuring (correctly) that it would take at least an hour for the extra-strength ibuprofen to kick in, three to get over my pain, and another three to get over the sight of my own blood, I called in a sick day. I also called my mom to pout.

4. They have special powers. I first noticed this in 6th grade, when I allowed a smile and a too-short-for-middle-school plaid skirt to convince me to pick the ridiculously endowed and hilariously uncoordinated Ericka White on my team for ultimate dodgeball. I saw it again a couple

---

[29] This also ties into a typical woman's capacity to be around and care for sick boyfriends. Seriously, I've always found it amazing that the same woman who needs to call the National Guard to help her kill a baby spider in her apartment will happily volunteer to spend the night with a guy with amoebic dysentery if she cares enough about him. –T.C.

summers ago, while waiting for a date to meet me outside of a Sushi restaurant in the Shadyside section of Pittsburgh.

It was raining, and a man in a business suit sprinted to a parked car a few yards away from me. Inside that car was a somewhat attractive January Jones—the actress who plays Don Draper's wife on "Mad Men"—doppelganger. When the guy reached the car, he pulled out what looked to be at least a couple hundred dollars and gave it to her through the window. Their conversation went as follows (paraphrasing):

Girl: *"Thanks, buddy. Things have been tight recently. I really appreciate it."*

Guy: *"Any time. Sorry for taking so long. I had to run to the ATM on Penn Avenue because the one on Walnut Street is out of order. So...what are you doing this weekend? I had some tickets to..."*

Girl speeds off in car while guy, literally still in mid-sentence, turns around and walks away

He then shot a shit-eating, *"Yeah, I know hot chicks. Jealous, aint you?"* grin at his buddies who were watching this entire exchange.

Let's forget the fact that they produce human beings. Let's also forget the fact that they're able to dance for seven consecutive hours in eight inch Nine West stilts without flinching. Being able to get away with shit like that *and have a man actually brag about it happening to him* is a superfuckinghuman ability.

80

Making Love in the Club...Or Not
21 Tips to Remember When Hitting the Club

By The Champ

While with a group of friends at a nightclub a few summers ago, I witnessed a terribly earnest and terribly awkward man approach of one my more attractive platonic (Ha!) lady friends. The guy was completely out of his league, and I cringed when anticipating the upcoming collision between his relative timidness and my homegirl's temerity. And, although I was already a good 15 feet away from my friend, I beelined to the bathroom; not wanting to witness the nightclub carnage.

I came back a few moments later and saw my friend holding a drink.

Champ: *"Well, that was quick."*
Friend: *"What do you mean?"*
Champ: *"I saw ole boy approach you a couple minutes ago. But, here you are, standing by yourself with a martini already."*
Friend: *"Well, he asked me if he could buy me a drink. I said yeah. He bought the drink, I told him it was nice of him to offer, and I told him to have a nice night."*
Champ: *"Ice cold! So basically, you told him to fuck off after he bought the drink?"*
Friend: *"Well, I didn't say fuck off. But...yeah. I didn't feel the need to talk to him."*
Champ: *"And you don't think there's anything wrong with that?"*
Friend: *"Huh? Hell no. Why should I?"*

What my homegirl failed to realize is that regardless of how aggressively un-cute or awkwardly devoid of swagger a guy might be, if he offers to buy a drink *and* you accept, you do owe him at least 60 seconds of conversation. Why? Well, it doesn't hurt to not be an asshole. Sure, ol' boy definitely could have approached my friend with a bit more confidence, but there would have been no harm in at least entertaining a conversation with him for a couple of minutes, *especially* after he spent money just to get an audience. Plus, by dismissing him so quickly, she likely ensured that she just made one person even more jaded and bitter about the dating process; basically the completely anti-thesis of the holistic *"happy people equals less crime"* Very Smart ideal.

Also, from a more personal standpoint, she had no idea who the hell she was talking to. For all she knew, Mr. Anti-swagger could be her boss in two months, the brother of the man she'll eventually marry, or the only guy who will happen to drive by when she blows out her tire on a deserted back road in a couple of months. It pays to be decent.

Of course, if he began the conversation by saying *"This martini is dry, isn't it? You know what I bet is the exact opposite? Your pussy,"* it would have been perfectly okay for her to throw the drink in his face and walk away. And, if he looked like Suge Knight, it would have been perfectly okay for her to throw the drink in his face and run away as fast as she could. Also, while we're still at the club...

1. Fellas, remember: women bartenders are like strippers. She's nice to you because she wants a bigger tip...just not the tip you have in mind. Don't be the asshole holding the orders up because you think you have a shot at bagging her.

2. If a woman is dancing while any of the following music is playing...

Dancehall reggae or soca. Bass music. House music (think of the type of music played on MTV's "Jersey Shore") Rap produced by Lil' John, Mannie Fresh, or Luther Campbell. Slow jams that could very easily be found on one of your college boning mixtapes.

...and makes eye contact with you, then it's perfectly okay to assume that she wants you to step behind her, and start grinding like you're the pepper boy and her name is mashed potatoes. Ladies, if any of these songs come on and you just want to dance with your girls and teasingly eye-fuck men, sit at the bar, grind on the stools, and don't write a 2000 word blog post the next day complaining about how men never approach you.

3. Fellas, if you ask a woman (a) to dance, (b) for her number, or (c) to buy her a drink and she declines, don't ask again, don't ask why, and definitely don't just stand behind her and wait for the song change to hopefully change her mind. Staying around like that will cause you to go from either *"guy I'm not interested in"* or *"guy I could be interested in, but this just isn't the right time"* to *"potential stalker who's going to make me get the bouncer in a couple more seconds"* in a moment's time. Find someone else, you fucking lame.

4. Fair or not, when you walk through that door you will be judged on your attire, your demeanor, the mean, median, and mode attractiveness of your crew, how

83

attractive you are in comparison to everyone else there, your drink of choice, and your walk. Each detail factors into your own personal baggability scale. If you can't reconcile yourself with these facts, stay home.

5. "Hi" and its myriad forms ("Hey," "Whats up?" "Hello," "How are you doing?" etc) is still the most reliable pick-up line, and her first response to the initial "Hi" is still the most reliable way of gauging sincere interest.

6. Ladies, if you're in a relationship, make sure to reveal that little tidbit in the first 15 to 45 seconds of conversation. Waiting longer than 60 seconds to drop the BF bomb officially makes you an asshole.

Seriously, spending an entire night laughing, dancing with, and getting to know a seemingly unbelievably compatible woman, only to be hit with the *"Hey, what type of movies do you like? I'm really into porn, Tarentino flicks, Scorsese, and old NBA highlight films. I love Spielberg films too, but not as much as my boyfriend does"* right before he's about to ask for her number should be enough for any guy to demand a club entrance fee refund directly from the woman's purse, and is easily one of the cruelest things that women do.[30]

---

[30] The single cruelest thing? **Keeping friend-zoned guys around**. Not only are most aware of the hapless friends they have who are patiently hoping for a never occurring opening, many of them have no problem with taking advantage of him once he's in place *and giving him just enough of a tease of a potential opening to keep him there*. My favorite is the wistfully nonchalant *"I wish there were more guys were like you. Why can't I find a good man?"* they'll utter to the emasculated cat driving them to IKEA so she can replace the bed her "maintenance man" just helped her break the night before. *−T.C.*

7. Everyone gets one *"I've had way too much to drink, and, if my crew doesn't step in I'm probably going to end the night either in jail or with an STD"* mulligan per every 9 months. Just one. After this, your crew doesn't have any more babysitting obligations.

8. Fighting isn't sexy under any circumstances. And by *"under any circumstances"* I mean *"unless a boob pops out."*

9. Fellas, it's probably not a good idea to be noticeably erect before you even dance with the chick. Getting noticeably hard during your personal grind session? Well, like sexual harassment, their reaction will basically depend on how attractive you are. My advice? Just try to have a big penis.

10. Ladies, if you want to get approached, separate from your crew and look like you're having a good time and they'll eventually come. It's really that easy. Also, leave your glasses **on.**[31] Not only do nice eyeglasses make you

---

[31] Angie Williams–*a high school classmate*–was the object of my silent appreciation for approximately three months in the spring of 1997, and my admiration completely stemmed from the fact that she was fucking *grown.* Not "grown" in the *"My 23 year old boyfriend is picking me up afterschool in his IROC"* way, but grown in the way you could imagine an 18 year old Claire Huxtable or Michelle Obama being. She had a general countenance and class about her that made her so far removed from the bullshit minutiae of high school existence that it was almost like she was a character in one of those teen movies where they cast 25 year old actors as high school sophomores and juniors. Even her usual daily "costume"–*black rimmed glasses, guess jeans, and a short, Halle Berry-esque 'do when most of the other girls had weave or ponytails*–gave more evidence to the idea that she belonged in a corporate office or courtroom instead of homeroom or study hall. I never said anything to her about the crush. But, she made such an impression on me that I've had a weakness for **women with glasses** ever since. *–T.C.*

even sexier than you already are, they serve as a screening technique because any man reluctant to approach you because of how "smart your glasses make you look" isn't the man for you. Plus, how else will you know if you gave your number to Denzel or Dragonface Derek?

11. Fellas, if you're old enough to get into the club, you're old enough to know by now that women at the club can be lemmings. Since you possess this knowledge, you should also be aware of the fact that if one member of a crew shoots you down, it decreases your chances of bagging someone else from that crew by 90%. Basically, pay attention and choose wisely.

12. Comfortable and club-appropriate clothing is a must. You don't want to be the person everyone is making fun of because you're sweating through your tuxedo or adjusting your seven-inches-too-short mini-skirt every three minutes.

13. Even if the drinks are free, always tip. Trust me, the bartender will appreciate it, and making friends with a bartender is a great, great gift that keeps on giving.

14. Unless you're at Caribana, Mardi Gras, or one of Diddy's all-white parties, once you're past 25, it's no longer acceptable to wait longer than 15 minutes or pay more than 20 bucks to get into any club.[32] If you sense

---

[32] While in Atlanta a couple years ago for Morehouse homecoming, my friends and I were at a lounge and, all of a sudden, the DJ cranked up the sound much to the chagrin and offense of everybody at my table. We were genuinely disturbed that they'd turn the music up so loud that we'd have to yell to speak to each other; so disturbed that we immediately left. And, this

that this is possible, go to another club or just go home. It's not that serious.

15. Regardless of what Usher says, there should be no making love in the nasty-ass club. That's what parking lots and IHOP bathrooms are for.

16. Ladies, make sure to leave with the exact number of people that you came with. If you want to hook up with a guy afterwards, go home first, or at least have one of your girls drive you to his spot. Drunkenly leaving the club with a stranger to hook-up is the intro for like 20% of the episodes of *"Law and Order: SVU."*

17. Fellas, once you're past age 21, knowing how to do any of the complex ringtone rap dances (Supaman, Lean With It Rock With It, etc.) officially makes you a lame, and potentially suspect. Luckily, there are some straight women who really dig suspect dudes, so knock yourself out, champ.

18. While dancing with someone, unless they're your significant other or Siamese twin, four songs should probably be the *"Hey, I'm gonna go check on my friends. I'll be back later"* dancing cut-off. Also, *"later"* should mean *"later on in the night,"* not *"when I get back from the bathroom"*

19. Fellas, unless your girl is actually there with you, if a woman approaches you and asks you to dance, always accept her offer.

---

is the exact moment I realized I was getting old. When you combine this with me turning into a *"Weekend Billboard"* (I've worn at least one piece of Morehouse clothing outside of my house every weekend since 2006) I'm definitely turning into my dad. –*P.J.*

20. If approaching a group of (three or more) women to offer drinks, you must either only buy a drink for the one you're specifically interested in, or the entire crew. No in-betweens. This...*"Bartender, get these three whatever they want. The other one, um, hmmm. Do you have any free corn chips or anything for her? ...*isn't cool. Funny? Definitely! But, not cool.

The Tenets of Grown-ass-ness

By The Champ

Go to any male-populated lunch table at pretty much any high school anywhere in the country, and there will be at least a 160% chance that the subject of conversation will pertain to something having to do with sex.

Even if they happen to venture off into another popular young male conversation topic (i.e.: *video games, Air Jordans, music, sports, cars, weed, etc*) within 5 to 10 minutes the subject will eventually turn back to something having to do with bragging in detail about the deed, creating some of the most hilariously awkward segues known to man.

"Yeah, man. Shaq is huge, man. I'd be scared to even try to...wait, wow, Kimberly...wow...did you see her today?? She'd definitely get the foot long Philly Cheese Steak, with all the toppings."

Because males at that age are so excited about the newly gained knowledge that their penises actually have a purpose other than waste disposal, this type of talk is excusable when coming from them.

With that being said, there's no quicker way to weed out **real men** from **immature assholes** than by using this rule: Grown-ass men don't brag about sex. It's crass, tactless, and extremely immature...which actually aren't bad qualities to hold if you're at the bar talking shit with your boys or playing ball. But, nothing screams *"I hate*

89

women" more than someone who constantly brags about what he does to them in the bedroom. Real men, manly men, don't brag, not about this at least, because that's what women are for. You don't volunteer information about how you "break backs" or how you're "packing a third leg." Let women you've been with in the past be your penis politicians. Trust me, many of them can't help themselves and they'd do it much better than we would anyway.

Anyway, while you'd probably get 10 different answers if you randomly asked 10 different people to define **grown-up** and explain exactly what a grown-up should do, I think we all can agree on what grown-ups—especially grown-ass men and women currently on the dating market—should never do.

1. Grown-ass women should never allow themselves to be solely defined by their sexuality. There's a fine line between *"sexy, sultry, and sensual"* and *"skanky, slutty, and smutty."* Wait, that's a lie. It is a very prominent and protruding line, a Grand Canyonesque line someone could see from miles away. If this line were typed on a sheet of paper, it would be in 72 pt font capital letters, underlined and *italicized* while in **bold**. Thing is, while there's a huge difference between sexy and slutty, the actual difference between them is created in a few very subtle characteristics.

None of these are more evident than the fact that women who look at their sexuality as a part of them tend to be the ones on the sexy side of the fence, while those who look at their sexuality as them, their sole defining trait, tend to venture more frequently into Skankville—the underground city subculture overwrought with red-light districts, clear heels, outrageously misfitting clothing, and outrageously misfitting perceptions of self-worth. Grown-ass women should know the difference.

A grown-ass woman should know that a long sleeved dress shirt, jeans, and an appropriate heel on her worst day still owns three times as much potential sexiness than some jeans revealing three inches of butt cleavage, accompanied by a fishnet turtleneck with pink piranha nipple clamps. A grown-ass woman should know that her sexuality will always be the implied and powerful elephant in the room and knows she doesn't need to acknowledge it by "yee-hawing" loudly and riding the elephant through the doorway like it's Seattle Slew.

Grown-ass women should also realize that as long as you treat your sexuality like the proverbial neon sign flashing "FOR AN UNLIMITED TIME ONLY, COME RIGHT HERE!!!!" on your back and between your legs, you'll continue to attract men who are only drawn to your billboards.

2. Grown-ass men should never try to "out-sexy" a woman. Unless you're an entertainer that gets paid for it, please don't ever try to "out-sexy" a woman. You can't do it, especially not if you need to try. The leather skinny jeans and extra snug Simon Cowell t-shirts, sticking your tongue out and constantly licking your lips, taking your shirt off for pictures...basically any type of sexy posing ever needs to stop. Now.

We're all are ugly and awkward. We can never be as outwardly sexy as a woman is, so stop trying. The things women do seem to find sexy in us aren't going to come across in a Facebook profile picture of you donned in tight spandex, sticking your ass out and smiling seductively on a chopper. Basically, try to look exactly how Bishop Eddie Long would look in a picture…only the exact opposite.[33] If I'm being too vague, here's a simpler way of seeing things:

Picture-wise, grown-ass men should limit themselves to three possible poses.

A) A content, closed or open mouth smile. This is to be used at weddings, family reunions, or company picnics; places where you're either genuinely happy to be there, or you're smiling just so you don't have to hear everybody complaining about you not smiling when they upload the pictures.

B) Jabberwocky. This is what I call the pose that happens when you're out with your boys or drunk and you end up taking some of the most hysterically disorderly pictures known to man. Jabberwocky pictures should also always make you shake your head and mutter "wow" to yourself in memory of the time they were taken.

C) A look of sheer and utter annoyance that someone has the audacity to try to take your picture.

3. Grown-ass men and grown-ass women should never get arrested or consistently put themselves in situations where it's a likely possibility. You're not T.I. or Lil' Kim or Martha Stewart. You have no albums to sell, movies to promote, or potato salad recipes to hawk. Your administrative-assistant-at-Blue Cross/Blue Shield ass

---

[33] Too soon? –*T.C.*

getting arrested is not cool and it will not enhance your "street cred." And, even if it did happen to enhance your status or "street cred," no other grown-ass man or grown-ass women is even going to care because you're an administrative assistant at Blue Cross/Blue Shield, and real gangstas don't work there.[34]

4. Grown-ass men should never leer (aka the "piss-boy pirouette"). You see this everyday: An attractive woman walks down a busy city sidewalk, and a few guys will react as if they're type-1 diabetics and a giant insulin-filled syringe is switching down the street.

At least once a month I'm either bumped into by a man still attempting to do the "over the shoulder, double take, blind walk" or even almost hit by a car driven by a man paying more attention to a pair of nice hips than the road and the man his car is about to hit. I bet at least 10% of man on man street skirmishes and car accidents are caused by prolonged leering. I once even saw a guy almost castrate himself after double-taking so intensely that he walked right into a fire hydrant.

---

[34] Real Gangstas also don't do each of the following things:

1. Read. If you're reading this, you're not a gangsta. Reading takes away from real gangsta activity. Gangstas don't read about murder, they're out doing it. And yes, comic books, Kool-Aid packets, street signs, contracts, newspapers, and the Qu'ran count.

2. Carry umbrellas. Gangstas don't give a shit about rain. True, nobody wants to get soaked, but you can't pull a .45 out, run, and then buck if you got an umbrella in one hand. How am I supposed to take your robbery attempt serious if you are really concerned about not getting wet while asking me for my wallet?

3. Lick ice cream cones. If I see you licking an ice cream cone and then you try to rob me, I just might be offended because that means you think I'm more pussy than you are. I might have to attempt to rob YOU on that premise alone. *—P.J.*

I'm not saying that you can't appreciate an attractive figure walking within eyesight, but always remember one thing: Act like you've seen it before. You don't want to be that guy. You know what guy I'm talking about. The guy who turns around and whistles and salivates at every woman he sees, regardless of the situation and/or circumstance.[35]

For a grown-ass man, not pirouetting and not making a fool of himself (and, in many cases, embarrassing the woman) in public is more important than getting in an extra three seconds of hip and switch peekage. A grown-ass man knows that he's seen it before and that he'll most likely see it again before the day is even over. Admire, don't ogle.

5. Grown-ass women should never hint at disinterest. It was much simpler in elementary school. If you liked a girl, you'd pass her a note in class with a simple question: Do you want to be on my team for dodgeball? Underneath the question would be two boxes, headed "yes" and "no." If she wasn't interested, not only would the "no" box get checked, you might even have the paper balled-up and thrown at you.

Somewhere in the 15 to 25 years after elementary school, many women have somehow come to the conclusion that instead of a concrete response, a hint of disinterest is all

---

[35] There's embarrassing, there's very embarrassing, there's uber embarrassing, and then there's the type of embarrassment that occurs when taking your new–and voluptuous–girlfriend to a family reunion and watching one of your uncles do the piss-boy pirouette every time she walks past. Actually, I'm lying. I wasn't embarrassed. She might have been, but I grinned from ear to ear every time I noticed it happening. Like uncle like nephew, I guess. –T.C.

that's needed to properly respond to unrequited romantic feelings. These women have seemingly forgotten one of the most basic rules every woman should know when dealing with a man: We are not women. By and large, we do not take hints. There's a reason why we sent the note in 3rd grade with "yes or no" checkboxes instead of a "maybe" or "sometimes." Unless we know the door is completely shut, we'll still think that we have a chance of getting in there somehow.

A grown-ass woman should know that if you're not romantically interested in a man, the best and most efficient approach should be to just tell him. Grown-ass women don't assume that he's going to eventually get the idea if they don't return his calls immediately, or if she only kisses him on the cheek, or if she never agrees to meet him somewhere if it's not daylight. A grown-ass woman should have enough figurative balls to be as honest with a man as possible, because she knows that doing it any other way is just wasting time for the both of you.

6. Grown-ass men and Grown-ass women should never, ever, ever have sex with any of the following people, unless you plan on marrying them: A direct superior at work. A staff person working directly underneath you at work. A sibling of a close friend. A close friend of a sibling. A mother, father, aunt, uncle, grandmother, grandfather, son, or daughter of anybody you know well. An ex of a close friend or family member. An unrequited long-time crush of a close friend or family member. A family member, unless you're near the Mason-Dixon line or the Everglades. Anyone who has ever worked in your home. A step-cousin. An ex-spouse or ex-fiancée. Anyone willing to have sex with you in their parents or

95

grandparents bed. A diehard Dallas Cowboy fan who's not from Dallas. A current student or teacher of yours. A former student or former teacher, if there's more than 10 years separating you two. Anyone who's more than double or less than half your age.

If this seems like a long list, just remember that there are roughly 7 billion people on the planet, and this has only eliminated maybe 75 of them; a small but worthy sacrifice on the never ending journey to Very Smartness.

Shady Hawkins Day
Why Women Shouldn't Hunt For Men

By The Champ

Apparently, the recession has been particularly hard on the feminists in my immediate social circle. They all seem to be moving out west for some reason. Maybe the 'Burgh just isn't very feminist friendly, who knows? This is unfortunate because it's always good to have a few radical feminists (*radfems*) in your sphere of influence. They make great drinking buddies because they love to buy rounds of rum and coke, they always have many interchangeable pairs of eyeglasses with angular frames, and they always seem to wear jeans without belts and carry purses full of Trader Joe's coupons.

In fact, as of this moment, I only have one remaining radfem buddy (and, I'm sure that'll change once she reads this chapter); a lawyer who usually hits me up once a month to get together so she can hear my take about her perpetual string of (her words) "wack-chunk relationships."

The last time we got together, she was uncharacteristically upset. Apparently, there'd been a distinct pattern with each of the last five or six guys she dated—initial red-hot intensity (read: "frequent and delirious sex") followed by the men becoming aggressively nonchalant and losing interest; a literal beginning *bang* and ending *whimper*—and she wanted some insight about why this pattern existed.

Now, although my radfem buddy is a radfem, she possesses all the stereotypical characteristics men

97

typically look for in women. She's smart as hell, funny, banging (*I'd even say she's the best looking white woman I've ever been cool with*[36]), and seems to enjoy talking about and having sex. Basically, she was the last person you'd think would have men *lose* interest, and I was curious to figure out why this was happening. This curiosity lasted for approximately two minutes, ending soon after I asked her one question:

"How do you typically meet guys?"

Her response—"*You know me. If I see someone I like, I pounce"*—told me everything I needed to know.

This, the **aggressive nonchalance,** is what usually eventually happens when women pursue men, which is why I've always maintained that *women should never do it.* Admittedly, most guys would probably say that I'm

---

[36] Since this—I'm a black man not shy about admitting an attraction for women who happen to be white—is true, you can probably assume I'm really just not that into black women. And, you'd be right to make that assumption. **Except, you wouldn't be. At all.** Despite what many seem to believe, a black man attracted to (or even *dating*) a white, or any other non-black, woman doesn't automatically mean he's not attracted to black women. In fact, it doesn't even mean he *prefers* white women. Saying "*I think Catherine Zeta-Jones is banging*" doesn't mean we don't think Nia Long, Sanaa Lathan, Gabby Union, Erykah Badu, Jill Scott, Nicole Beharie, Esther Baxter, Res, Sharon Leal, Tamron Hall, Swin Cash, Rissi Palmer, and Aisha Tyler are even banginger (I know that's not a word, but bare with me).

"*I think some white women are attractive*" and "*I'm completely enamored and in love with black women*" aren't mutually exclusive concepts. In fact, they're the complete opposite of mutually exclusive, they're, um, whatever the complete opposite of "mutually exclusive" happens to be. —*T.C.*

nuts for saying this, that they wish more women approached instead of just standing patiently in the weeds with their thumbs up their finely coiffed asses, and that there's no bigger ego boost than getting propositioned by an attractive (and sober) woman. I understand that sentiment, because I feel the exact same way.

Thing is, from a relationship standpoint, a woman making the first move usurps one of a man's most basic duties: *To show a woman that he has enough balls to approach her.* Stripping us of that can give us the idea that things will be excessively easy and strips the women of one of natures inherent bitchassedness filters. How the hell is he going to protect her from lions, tigers, bears, and crackheads if he couldn't even muster a weak "Hi" while behind her in line at Starbucks?

Also, the aggressive nonchalance typically occurs because he's probably not really all that interested. If he was, he would have approached *her first.* You see, women usually don't *grow* on men; at least not in the same way that a man can grow on women. While men typically are given a chance to prove if we're worthy enough to be taken seriously, men usually evaluate a woman's *worthiness* when we see her for the first time. If she doesn't immediately make the cut then, she probably won't ever. Basically, if we don't think you were attractive enough to approach to begin with, we'll probably never think that you're attractive enough to actually have a committed relationship with you. This is how women eventually get *Close-Bused* (more on this in Chapter 17).

Now, I'm not saying women don't have a part in this. Just as it's our job to approach if we're interested, *it's their job* to make themselves somewhat approachable if they're interested. Smiling, eye contact, *starting conversations*, subtly making your relationship status clear, responsive body language; all of this is perfectly within a women's wheelhouse. But, unless you just want a couple rolls in the hay, walking up to him and saying, *"Hey, I've been noticing you for a while and I think you're sexy. Lemme have your number,"* is not the way to go

Honestly, I've never actually seen it work. Yeah, I seen situations where they may have dated a few times and exchanged some seminal fluid for a while, but I've never actually heard any first-hand testimony from a long-standing couple who initially met when the woman bagged her boyfriend or husband. Not once.

Of course, I told my radfem buddy all of this. And, of course, she didn't listen to any of my advice. An hour or so later, she actually approached a guy at the bar who she thought looked like a *"hotter, younger, and straighter Anderson Cooper."* She'll learn eventually. If not, well, I'm always up for another round.

Trickeration
How to Get a Date at the Last Minute (When Being You Hasn't Been Quite Good Enough)

By Panama Jackson

As The Champ stated in "19 Things About Sex I Definitely Didn't Learn in Sex-Ed," it's usually not the best idea to date desperately. And, as I found out last summer, it's also usually not a great idea to battle an overflowing septic tank with a single bottle of Febreze. Not a good look, and definitely not a good smell.

Excessively shitty situations aside, sometimes even the most charming and delightful dater can hit a rough patch where they need a date to an upcoming event (i.e.: a wedding, a company picnic, a high school reunion, an evening carjacking, etc) but their usual charms have been rendered ineffective by a prolonged cold spell. And, like with a faulty septic tank, sometimes you don't have time to inspect the plumbing or call a plumber. Sometimes a prayer and a bottle of Febreze are your only options, and here are a few ways you can temporarily Febreze yourself out of loneliness.

1. Bullshit. Just walk up to the object of your desire and strike up a conversation about something you know very little about, but are able to bullshit about well. Hopefully, this should be a subject most people are aware of, but don't have a complete grasp of either. Jazz usually works, but health care reform and Toni Morrison novels work even better.

Also, and this is specific to the fellas, start a conversation about how you'd like to make a difference in the world and how your life really isn't about you. While doing this, try to use as many song lines, titles, and prepositional phrases in your conversation as possible *and* try even harder to make sure all of your references are from somewhat obscure 70's soul albums. Citing Marvin Gaye is great, but Boz Scaggs is a little bit better.

2. Don't be yourself! For instance, let's say you're a garbage man. Well, clearly that doesn't sound sexy to the women sitting at the bar. With that resume, most folks would probably tell you to call yourself a sanitation engineer. I'll do you one better! Tell her you're a lawyer. You might not ever see her again anyway, so who gives a shit? Hell, tell her that you're working reparations but can't talk about it because it's a pending case.

For women, just tell random men that you were born to be a housewife and cater to your man[37]. Hell, tell him that you have the song "Cater 2 U" by Destiny's Child

---

[37] The three sexiest occupations?

1. **Grade School Teacher.** Their occupation forces them to be ultra-sensitive, tireless, well-rounded, and flexible, and I assume that this ultra-sensitivity, tirelessness, well-roundedness, and flexibility is applicable in other areas.

2. **Yoga Instructor.** I know the inclusion of "yoga instructor" on this list is about as predictable as a Tyler Perry movie. I also know that I've never actually met a woman who teaches yoga, and no one within my sphere of influence has either. Shit, I'm not even completely sure that women yoga instructors or yoga itself actually exists.

3. **Librarian.** Like Canadians and 40-something strippers, librarians always seem to have a naughty twinkle in their bespectacled eyes. While the cause of the perpetual eye fuck could very easily be dust from the 1994 World Book encyclopedias they had to archive that morning, I think that they're spending most of their days sitting there day-dreaming about black cowboys and cocoa butter, and the twinkle is equal parts annoyance at being interrupted, embarrassment at being caught, and invitation. –*T.C.*

on repeat on your iPod and that it has been adopted as your theme song.

3. Do the exact opposite of what you'd normally do! Just like with #2, essentially go out of your way to be the complete opposite person of who you are usually. If you're normally quiet, be the center of attention somewhere and draw the men/women into your web of deception. If you're a nice guy, make sure the woman you're interested in sees you stab someone.

In fact...

4. Be the brother who looks pitiful because his wife, girlfriend, or dog just left him! As the thousands of women sitting in county jail lobbies everyday proves, there are few things chicks love more than a fixer-upper, and nothing says *"Please help me"* better than a dude who looks like he's been scorned by every black woman in Baltimore. Go to the bar and put on a show. Make sure that the women notice you, but act like you don't notice them noticing you. Make it seem like your world is coming to a complete and total end. Talk to yourself. Have angry conversations with yourself that start with, *"I should have KNOWN...."* Loudly confess to your own stupidity at least three times and make sure that the women hear you. Tell her that you're not good enough for her. You have to really sell this shit though. You can't just act pathetic, you have to BE pathetic.

In fact, pretend that your best friend just slept with your mother. That should fuck you up REAL good! (Sorry, Lebron.)

Oddly enough, this doesn't work for women. While (some) men do relish their *Captain Save a Ho* titles, you won't find too many with the *Captain Save a Depressed and Borderline Suicidal Woman* moniker. (Unless, of course, you happen to be a light-skinned male character in a Tyler Perry movie.)

5. If you're a woman, just put 'em on the (figurative) glass. I guarantee you'll get some attention and a date. Just remember that you'll now have a plethora of dates to choose from, but that sounds like one of those good problems to me. If you're blessed with no chest, just carry a Playboy around with you and flash those instead. Dumb men won't know the difference, and we're not exactly looking for Mensa candidates, are we?

6. Men, take books with you everywhere. Extra points if you go to a bar or lounge or somewhere where people usually aren't supposed to be reading. Personally, I'd suggest Applebee's or a wake. If you look friendly enough, some woman will ask you about the book you're reading. If you're able to say something about it, you're guaranteed some conversation, and probably enough to seal the deal.

7. Use poetry. You don't have to get all Taylor Mali or Nikki Giovanni on us. Just say something simple like...

"My love for you is like a river. Like a summer breeze that makes my soul shiver. One look from you is more precious than gold...let's go get some barbecue and get busy!!!!"

...to a random person in line at Target, and you'll be in like Flynn. Bonus points if you smell like Patchouli.

8. Let everyone know how great your credit is.[38] A long time ago (read: last summer), I came up with the idea to get a t-shirt made that said, *"I'm A Black Man With Good Credit,"* in big bold letters. On the back would be my actual credit score number, with a giant yellow smiley face directly underneath it. I never actually made that shirt, but a shirt like this would definitely help a struggling brotha get some attention at the bar. Who knows? Maybe you'll end up dating one of the dozen or so women who'll ask you to co-sign on a car loan.

9. Volunteer. Do you know what really warms my heart? Blankets, puppies, and fat strippers. Do you know what warms the hearts of many, if not most, women? A man who cares about other people. I used to volunteer at a high school in D.C., and I can't tell you how many women were in there helping out. How many Black men? Two. It was a veritable buffet of liberal, pot smoking idealists with big hair, non-profit salaries, and a willingness to discuss revolution while lying naked on your futon. Your only requirement is to not mess it up.

10. Be funny. Funny men—even funny-looking funny men—can always meet women. If he's just funny by nature, he'll stay winning because women like smiling. It just touches a part of them that makes them want to do happy things and say happy sayings.

---

[38] By the way, if your credit score is the same as your age, reading this book probably won't increase it very much. But, if you do happen to go to a bank for a loan, make sure you take a copy of the book with you. The loan officer will definitely be impressed with the sound financial decision you made when buying this, and that should definitely help your chances. —*P.J.*

11. Start a blog, and wear a t-shirt with the name of your blog everywhere you go. As the love lives of The Champ and I prove, nothing seems to make previously uninterested women interested in you more than if they find out you've founded a blog. And, as the vast majority of the internet proves, the blog itself doesn't even have to be any *good*; all you need to do is update it twice a month with tales of your relationship woes, and make sure to be seen wearing the t-shirt with the name of the blog whenever there's a chance someone might take a picture of you.

If this doesn't work, you can always just tell women you're writing a book.

Salt Your Own Sack
How We (Men) Have Perfected the Fine Art of Being Our Own Worst Enemy

By The Champ and Panama Jackson

Depending on where you get your information, it apparently takes somewhere between 5 and 55 seconds for a woman to decide whether a man she just met is potential mating material. Thing is, between that first interaction and the second Thanksgiving you've spent with her folks, we have an annoying tendency to stupidly make dating and relationship missteps that'll give her no choice but to pursue new partners. Usually, these mistakes aren't even major deal-breakers like infidelity, domestic violence, and wearing white tube socks with dress shoes or sandals, but just little grains of salt sprinkled so frequently that they'll eventually ruin the entire meal.

Split into two groups—*"How To Destroy Your Dating Life, Dumb-Ass"* and *"How To Ruin Your Relationship, Retard"*—here are a few of our most common faux pas.

Part 1: How To Destroy Your Dating Life, Dumb-Ass

1. Be too nice. While genuine interest from a woman doesn't give you carte blanche to be an asshole, nothing makes a woman go from Brazilian Rainforest to Sahara Desert quicker than excessive and unconditional niceness. Seriously, sacrificing your spine before you get the panties is such surefire anti-damp that you might as well change your name to Bounty.

It's not that women abhor niceness. In today's cutthroat dating game, a genuinely nice guy is usually appreciated and admired, a breath of fresh air in an otherwise toxic battlefield. But, being too nice, too willing, and too accommodating all of the time is a bit creepy.

If you're not exactly sure what constitutes *too nice*, just follow the same simple dating Do's and Don'ts that **successful assholes**—men and women whose usual dating success is directly related to the fact that they refuse to appease just for appeasing's sake—tend too.

A) Don't be afraid to be yourself. What makes assholes attractive to many is their unflinching confidence in themselves, and the fact that they don't allow circumstance to dictate who they are. If the typical *too nice* guy is a chameleon, the asshole is a **grizzly bear**; scratching his balls while bitch-smacking mountain lions and throwing raw salmon at women he's trying to get into the cave.

B) Don't be scared to show your passion. While tooting your own horn may not be in your nice guy nature, if you're a crocheting ass ninja, don't be scared to let everyone know that you'll thread the shit out of a shower curtain.

C) Don't settle for friendship. You already have enough friends. What the hell do you need another for, especially one who's made it clear that there's no chance of romantic reciprocation? If you're interested in a woman, and she's given you a romantic rain check after you've made your intentions known, fuck staying around as a lame-duck friend, and burn that dry-ass bridge and never look back, bitch.

D) Do limit the self-depreciating humor. Because they're generally non-confrontational by nature, making people as relaxed and comfortable around them as possible to avoid potential conflict is deeply embedded in the nice guy DNA. The best way to do this is to make yourself seem non-threatening, and the quickest and easiest way to appear non-threatening is to laugh at yourself.

Thing is, while a little self-depreciation is good, hosting a daily solo roast of yourself and your flaws will make it extremely difficult for anyone to take you seriously. Plus, if you're perpetually pin-pointing and joking about your imperfections, eventually *your flaws are all anyone's going to notice.*

E) Don't act like anyone is out of your league. Of course, some women will think they're too good for you. Some might even give you a *"How dare you think you can even talk to me?"* sneer while they're taking your order at Wendy's. But, assholes don't concern themselves with people who don't want them and you shouldn't either. Fuck her (figuratively and literally) and her lukewarm fries (just figuratively).

F) Do be interesting once people are paying attention to you. And, by "interesting" we mean, "be you;" the you that's charming—even if that charm is just plain ole crocheting goofiness. Getting them to notice you is half the battle. Now you have to give them a reason to actually stay.

G) Don't let anyone you're interested in hook you up with a friend. Basically, if a woman hits you with the...

"Hey, bud. Even though I think you're great, we will never, ever, ever be a romantic match. On the bright side, I have a much less attractive friend who, if you both can ever get past the fact that I'm passive-aggressively implying that I'm better than her because I think she might be into someone I've personally found repulsive, might be a good match for you. Are you interested?"

...throw a stink bug at her.

H) Do *compete*. While you shouldn't have to *openly* pursue for another person's affection, remember that every person, unattached or attached,[39] is in indirect competition for each other. Basically, you need to bring something to the table other than just being a nice person. Assholes know this, and aren't scared to do what it takes to get what they want. Shit, leather couches are nice, but we'll continue to sit, sleep, spill shit, and fart on them until one of them gives us a convincing reason to date 'em.

It took the Young Champ a while to know this, as he had a tendency to take sexual interest as a cue to instantly turn into Stuart Smalley[40]; so worried about not doing anything to upset his potential partner that he neglected

---

[39] The competition doesn't end when you're in a relationship. You may not be actively looking, but *both you and your mate are still on the market*. Just because you made the team doesn't mean you should stop working on your game. Rest assured, your starter status won't stop hungry-ass free-agents from trying to take your spot. –T.C.

[40] Yes, I'm fully aware of how I dated myself with that **Stuart Smalley**–*The "I'm good enough, I'm smart enough, and doggone it, people like me!" guy from Saturday Night Live*–reference. Thanks for asking, though. –T.C.

to continue being the person the potential was actually interested in. He was the football team playing *not to lose* instead of trying to **win**, not realizing that always bending over backwards is a great way to make sure you won't be breaking any backs any time soon.

Plus, being too willing to be held hostage to each of her whims gives most women the impression that you're pandering for panties[41] instead of actually interested in her.

2. Act like you're already in there. Even if they know you know they want to sleep with you, women still like to be wooed as if you're completely oblivious to the soggy circus jumping out of her jean suit. With that being said, unless you're Carmelo Anthony or Johnny Depp, it's usually not the best idea to assume that sex is a sure thing. Trust, saying *"It's about fucking time"* or *"I knew you couldn't resist the King"* when she finally decides to join you for a nightcap usually doesn't go over as well as faux surprise and genuine appreciation does.

---

[41] "Panty-pandering" definitely makes the cut on the list of "Subtle Signs That He Ain't Shit", along with:

1. He always refers to women as "females." While the word female is appropriate under certain contexts, beware of the cat that uses it as his universal descriptor of all women. Honestly, I have absolutely no idea why this is such a strong indicator of ain't-shitness. But, every guy I've known who regularly incorporates female in their daily lexicon in lieu of other appropriate substitutes (woman, chick, earth, concubine, etc.) has been an ain't shit dude, so go figure.
2. He's a grown-ass man with abs. While certain professions (professional athlete, physical trainer, guido, stripper, etc.) make sculpted abdominal muscles a reasonable and practical asset, the fact that our metabolism slows as we age means that a grown-ass man with artificially enhanced abs is probably too obsessed with himself (and sleeping with other men) to give a damn about you. Also, if this all just sounds like a bunch of thinly-veiled haterade, good. Mission accomplished. –T.C.

With this in mind, you should also probably kill the overly lascivious lingo as well. While some women do actually enjoy excessive forwardness, the safest route is to just assume that your second date probably isn't the time to tell her you're going to break her back in half or that her breasts look like two tasty chocolate puppies.

3. Reveal your inner "metro." Recently, the inane "down-low" hysteria—when J.L. King's book, *"The Down Low,"* made pretty much every black woman in America suspicious that any straight man she met was also pitching for the pink team—has quelled somewhat since it's circa 2004 high point. With that being said, women (black women especially) are still extra vigilant for any signs of pre- or immediately post-coital effeminacy, and excessive amounts of it can quickly change the scenario from *"Hmm. Maybe I can be his girlfriend"* to *"Hmm. He'd definitely make a great girlfriend."*

Unless you plan on dozens of consecutive nights of lonely solo exfoliation, archive the colored contacts and timely celeb gossip until at least the third time you've slept together, Farnsworth.

4. Full-court press as soon as the game starts. While mysteriousness can be sexy, we all still like to have some inkling of reciprocation, women especially. It's no fun being interested in someone who's loathe to express any interest in you, and there's nothing wrong with letting a woman know that you're pleased with how things are currently progressing between you two. With that being said, sometimes we have a tendency to take the whole *"I like you, too"* thing a bit too far, and that shit can get scary.

Shifting your busy schedule to spend time with her? Good reciprocation.

Sending her a note/text/voicemail/email letting her know how much you enjoyed your last date and that you're looking forward to seeing her again? Great reciprocation.

Offering to pay her phone bill, updating your Facebook status message to say "*I've found her,*" and taking her to the grave of your beloved great-grandmother to pray for her blessing....after your first date? Bad, bad, bad reciprocation. Down, boy. Down, dammit!

5. Let her see you "sleeping". If you're a grower—a man whose flaccid penis is less than half of its erect size—you should remember that there are many women who've made it to adulthood without ever seeing adult shrinkage. In fact, you could wager that at least 15 to 25% of the women reading this are unaware it even exists. First impressions definitely matter, and since good sex for a woman usually has just as much of mental component as a physical one, her being unable to shake the fact that her first view of your hog reminded them of a pig's tail probably isn't a good thing.

Basically, while you may be carrying around a fully-loaded Philly cheese steak sub when erect, it's not the best idea to whip out your sleeping wang if it resembles a Steak-umm while soft. Shit, if she told you she was going to make you a burger, you probably wouldn't want to see her actually kill the cow, right? Well, same concept.

6. Get your ass kicked in front of her. Regardless of her beliefs about gender equality, Patriarchy, and Robin Givens, pretty much every woman would prefer to be with a man who makes them feel safe and secure. Nobody wants to date the brotha who makes them feel like they'll have to jump into his fight because he can't handle his own, and it's doubtful that *"Remember that time last year when my man got knocked the fuck out at Baby Foot Locker?"* is a topic most women want to bring up while chatting with their girls.

And, with all the money they spend on hair and other beauty products, their being loath to actually fight is perfectly understandable. [42]

So what if you're one of those cats who really, really, really *means* it when they say, *"I'm a lover, not a fighter"*? What if "you" and "fighting" go together about as well as "T.I." and "freedom"? Your woman still has to feel safe doesn't she?

Well, here are a few ways to fake it 'til you make it, guaranteeing that you'll never have to fight to defend your girls honor.

A) Only eat at restaurants frequented by older and/or non-black patrons with something to lose. Basically, TGIFridays and Applebee's are totally out, and even The Cheesecake Factory is pushing it if in Atlanta or Chicago. You should probably just stick to sushi bars and Thai restaurants.

Of course this might hurt your pockets and require you to know which one is the salad fork, but it's a small price

---

[42] Unless of course, she's a hoodrat. In which case, she might instigate a fight that you have no way of winning. Some unsolicited advice? After your 19th birthday, don't date hoodrats. The adventure just isn't worth it. Also, never date a woman with an intentionally visible tattoo of her name on her neck, wrists, or teeth. That also isn't a good look. –P.J.

to pay. She won't know that you're a punk, she won't suspect that you're not able to hold your own, and you just improved your etiquette. Plus, you'll get *nice restaurant* points from her, which means she'll be more likely to stay in and cook for you for the next date, which means less chance of getting your ass kicked.

Also, this is one of the few times when young black males can use the fact that many people will be scared of them just because they're young and black to their advantage. Even if you're the anti-Deebo, try to take advantage of one of the few perks of living in a not so post-racial country.

B) Stay away from places where young people congregate. It's a well known fact that young people are tantamount to senseless violence. Youth breeds ignorance and ignorance breeds fisticuffs, and you need to stay away from that type of breeding if you want to do some of the fun breeding.

C) Be extremely funny and personable. It's hard to fight the funny guy. Everybody knows that humor is the best defense against ignorance. Actually, that's not true at all, but it looks very reassuring in print. However, being funny generally guarantees that you won't get into too many arguments. Mind you, be funny, not an asshole. Assholishness exponentially increases your beat-down probability. You want to stay on the lower end of that confidence interval.

Plus, if you're funny and personable, you'll probably date a woman who's at least similar in nature and neither of you will find yourselves shouting down a car with four men with Dickies' jumpsuits and neck tattoos because they cut you off.

115

D) Be proactive, like the Black Panthers (not like Diddy or Jessica Simpson). This requires you to be a little bit smarter than the average bear, or at least have some foresight. If you see a situation that could even remotely get out of control, you have to squash it before that happens. On the other hand, if it's your girl's fault—she decided to scream at somebody because they were *"looking at her like they knew her"* (*which is hoodrat behavior, by the way*) —then just leave her ass exactly where you found her. Hopefully she doesn't know where you live.

E) Date chicks no one else really wants. You probably won't have to ever fight for your woman's honor if people are happy as hell that you're the damn fool who took her off the market.

F) Have enough family and friends with sketchy pasts to do all of your dirty work for you. Of course, this requires them to be on call 24/7, and for them to be able to get there at the drop of a hat, which is highly unlikely. However, if this is at all possible, make it so. This way, you can protect your brand (and record) and your loyal-to-a-fault family can exercise their ignorance. It's a win-win for everybody involved.

And, if your girl wonders why you always get other people to fight your (physical) battles, leave her. She's probably a hoodrat.

Part 2: How to Ruin Your Relationship, Retard

Even after we've successfully thwarted the dating and courting Kraken and somehow managed to convince a woman we're relationship worthy, there still remains a few things we can do to put our days of playing the *pull-out game* with her on permanent pause.

1. Give the wrong damn gift all of the time. Ever since Adam made the mistake of buying Eve a mammoth skin handbag for Valentine's Day when she specifically asked for vintage velociraptor, knowing what and what not to purchase a woman has been one of the toughest questions for a man to ponder.

Although women's inherent schizophrenia ensures that we'll probably never know exactly what to get her, you should be straight as long as you make sure that you stay as far away as possible from the following ideas.

A) Your dick in the inbox. Actually, this applies to all unsolicited pictures, even the PG ones. Randomly sharing those Droid camera pictures you took in the mirror last week that show off your goatee is one of the quickest ways to go from *"He's cool"* to *"He's cool, but I think he likes nuts on his chest."*

Plus, some women are unrelenting size queens. So, while you might think your penis is above average and praiseworthy, remember that *average* is a relative term and that your *above average* could very easily equal a months worth of jokes at your expense with the right set of chicks.

B) A new gym membership and any other out of the blue workout paraphernalia. While it's perfectly okay to renew gym memberships or purchase track shoes and treadmills for your girl if she's already a workout fanatic, bringing up even the faintest hint that she needs to hit the gym—or anything else that suggests she might need to lose weight—is a bad idea on par with *"Wow. That raccoon is so cute. I wonder if it can fit in my mouth."*

C) Crabs. Although herpes is the gift that keeps on giving, crabs creates a cruel and confusing conundrum because of the obvious permanent negative imagery it gives women who love seafood. Basically, while the big "H" might stall her horse riding and nude sailing days— at least according to the ubiquitous Valtrex commercials—the coochie crabs will ruin Red Lobster forever, and we know how much women love Red Lobster.

D) An abortion. Hey Capitan! When she asked you to be more considerate about sex, sending her a *"Hey, babe. How was your day? After work, let's head down to the abortion clinic. I heard they're having a special this week, and there's a Chick-fil-A right around the corner"* text in the middle of the day probably isn't what she had in mind.

E) Clothes from any store with a "one-size for all" plastic bag. Let's put it this way: If you're buying her a Very Smart Brothas baby-tee and the sales clerk stuffs it in the same six gallon garbage bag perps use to hide dead hookers on *"CSI: Miami,"* the thought still counts, but she probably won't give a fuck.

It's okay for her to hunt for clothes at bargain basement stores for sales and deals. But, if you're thinking about buying her something she actually wants to wear, knowing that you copped it on a clearance rack at a store that also sells produce and HDTV stands is a surefire way to go from being *"that nigga"* to *"guess what that triflin' nigga tried to buy me?"* for at least a year.

118

F) Lotion, tampons, douche, or a new brand of deodorant or soap. Unless you're training for a marathon and you're intentionally aiming for three straight months of desert dick, you probably don't want to give the implication that your woman could use a bit more help with her sanitary and scent game. Even though this gift idea is definitely practical and definitely shows that your heart is in the right place, you'd actually be in less trouble if you just threw a bottle of baby powder at her.

G) Anything she can use to efficiently plot your demise. This includes guns, cutlery, account passwords, bleach, razors, pre-sharpened pencils, darts, the *Dexter* DVD box set, secrets about your family, handcuffs, whips and chains, and nude pictures of your better looking ex.

H) Weave. While many black (and non-black) women enjoy the fruitful pleasures of lace fronts, extensions, and other types of artificially enhanced hair we know absolutely nothing about, it's probably not the best idea to give your girlfriend a big ol' bag of Indian hair as a surprise birthday gift unless you want her to beat you with it.

2. Continue to hit the club. Show us a man in a serious relationship who still goes clubbing twice a week and we'll show you a man hanging for dear life on the edge of the cheating cliff. Why? Well, from the fact that guys pay for entrance fees and drinks while women have *"Free before midnight"* and *"Ladies with orange thongs drink for free"* deals, to the perpetual radio, TV, and flyer nightclub promotions featuring nothing but women as their main attraction, clubs are places specifically designed for men to come and see as many women in one place as possible.

Because of this, a man doesn't go clubbing to chill with his boys or to dance. If we're consistently at the club, and it's not related to our occupation in some way, it's to find chicks to bag and bone. That's it. There's no other reason. We're just not built to be able to rub up against scantily clad and lascivious hoochies and not want to get her number or buy her a drink or a BMW.

Plus, from sports bars and fantasy sports to barbershops and BBQs, we have tons of other opportunities to bond with each other. Night clubs ain't for bonding or chillin. They're for booty and booty potential; two things a relationship minded man shouldn't have on his radar.

Oddly enough, strip clubs don't count.

In fact, women should be happy if their man and his boys hit nudie bars instead of nightclubs because there's pretty much no chance in hell he'll be able to "bag" one of the strippers, regardless of how much he might think he wants to. Sure, his pockets will be a little lighter and he'll probably come home with the "SCOO"[43] (Strip-Club Odd Odor), but he'll definitely be coming back home that night, and that's all that matters.

3. "Window shop" exactly the same way. A few years ago, there was a woman who worked in the perfume section of a department store in downtown Pittsburgh who happened to have the best butt-to-waist ratio The Champ had ever seen. As a self-proclaimed connoisseur of curvy woman, The Champ felt it was his duty to find a

---

[43] I've been trying to figure out the mixture of smells that contributes to the SCOO, and I've come to realize that it's a combination of ass sweat, recycled bacon grease, Nair, MD 20/20, old pennies, Bath & Body Works' Cucumber Melon Fragrance Mist, more ass sweat, and struggle. *–T.C.*

way to position himself so that he had a clearer view of her every time he entered the store; sometimes even feigning to *look for stuff for his sister's birthday* just to get a better view. He wasn't malicious. He had no intent on picking her up or even flirting with her; he just wanted a better view of a once in a lifetime viewing experience. Problem was, he was in a relationship at the time, and he also knew that there'd be times in the near future when he was in that store with his girlfriend. This created a great dilemma: How would he perform his connoisseur duty without offending his girlfriend?

He anguished about it for days until it hit him...**just tell her about the woman!** Women get fascinated by stuff like that too, just differently. While we're thinking, *"DAMN, LOOK AT THAT ASS!!!"* they're thinking *"Damn, I wonder where she buys jeans to fit her proportions. They must cost her a fortune. She must have her own tailor. Wait, how can she afford to have her own tailor if she's working at Macy's? She's probably a stripper at night."* He told his girlfriend about the woman behind the perfume counter with the great behind, and the next time they went into the store together, he pointed her out saying, *"Look!!! There she is. I told you it was unique."* She responded, *"Wow that really is amazing. I wonder if she has trouble sitting down."* Problem solved.

Now, if it's a spontaneous looker walking down the street while you're with your girl, you can always say *"Would you wear an outfit like that?"*, or even better, *"Wow. It's like 50 degrees outside. Why the hell is she wearing that tiny top? You can even see her nipples. Skank."* Of course your girlfriend is going to agree and join in with her own snarky comments while you continue to get your gaze on.

121

Perfect this and you'll never get the cold "*I caught you looking at her*" shoulder again.

4. Continue to converse with your sworn enemy (other women) as if they weren't your sworn enemy. (A relatively harmless random Gmail chat conversation between a single man and a woman acquaintance)

Woman: "*You know what? I've been really horny for some reason recently. It's like I've been fantasizing about every man that I see.*"

Man "*Word? Damn. Expound. What do you mean? Explain, please. In detail.*"

(A relatively harmless random Gmail chat conversation between a man in a relationship and a woman acquaintance)

Woman: "*You know what? I've been really horny for some reason recently. It's like I've been fantasizing about every man that I see.*"

Man: "*You crazy. Did I tell you about this great omelet I made this morning?*"

Woman: "*Did you make your omelet with a heated skillet? Just asking because I've been trying to find a way to incorporate one in the bedroom. Did I ever tell you about the time in the Greyhound station bathroom with the Dominican twins...*"

A man in a serious, committed relationship needs to quickly figure out one thing:

Most women are assholes, assholes who—if aware you're in a happy relationship—will subtlety mention some "innocent" sexual detail whenever they get an opportunity, just to fuck with you.

Honestly, we don't think they can even help it. In fact, we actually believe that they have clandestine national meetings underneath Williams-Sonoma every other weekend to discuss which one of us is in a relationship.

At approximately 4:26 pm Eastern Standard Time last Sunday, James Jackson of Albany, New York, proposed to his longtime girlfriend, and we need to test him before he makes his vows. He's particularly vulnerable between 12:25 and 12:50 Wednesday afternoons, right before he has his lunch. Kim, since he has a thing for leggy women, and is particular about his cologne, we're going to need you to slide up to him in line at Wendy's this week and compliment his new Kenneth Cole Black. He also has a thing for business women, so make sure to wear your sexiest pant suit. A slight French accent would be cool too, since he's infatuated with Haitians.

Even though it's innocent and you have no intentions on stepping outside of the relationship, the conversations about *horniness, horseback riding,* and *lotioning* cannot be co-signed. Every response must be a literal "SMH" (Shaking My Head), followed by *"You crazy and shit."* That's it. Don't ask, don't inquire, don't even respond with a smiley face, or you'll be sliding down the vaginal wetness induced slippery slope of cheating.

5. Fail to realize that our version of "Hope and Change" is an unrealistic and unfair pipe-dream. Despite what's commonly thought, we actually fall in love much faster than women do.[44]

But, this feeling has a tendency to freeze like a broken DVD player; a "love" somewhat dependent on our **hope** that women never, ever, ever, ever **change** anything. Although we're aware of time and biology and nature and shit, sometimes we still stupidly expect them to stay the exact same perpetually horny, bubbly, and perky 24 year old they were when we first saw them, with the exact same hair, occupation, personal outlook, income, and libido.

Trust us when we tell you that this tendency to hold women to that unrealistic and unfair expectation is the impetus behind most male-inspired relationship acrimony.

6. Forget that the absence of very bad shit doesn't automatically equal a good relationship. We can't help it. We're victims. Slaves to our own stories. Helpless to our own hype.

You see, we've all been led to believe that a relationship devoid of serious jankyness automatically equates to great mate and happy chick. While the rest of the world wades through the shallow muck of relationship murk, many of us feel that by simply *not* cheating and *not* beating her ass, we should be entitled to constant blow jobs and on-demand Cream of Wheat whenever we're famished. This feeling leads to complacency, making us

---

[44] This is definitely true. For every woman reading this, every man who's ever fallen in love with you probably started falling before you even told him your name. My point? Despite our claims to the contrary, we're just as fucking batshit crazy as you are. –T.C.

occasionally forget about that just being there and not fucking up isn't enough to make her happy.

7. Never let her in. Many, if not most, men are loathe to speak on shit that's bothering us, especially in regards to relationships. We relish being the "strong, silent" type, and revel in the props, praise, pussy, and premature pulmonary hypertension that comes with it. Sometimes though, these relationship "bothers" we loath to speak on continue to fester and grow, culminating with a sneak attack *"I haven't been happy for six months"* evening dumping seemingly out of left field.[45]

I'm not saying that we need to start going all Kanye and shit. There's nothing worse than a complaining ass man. Okay, that's a lie. A complaining ass man with a lisp and sporadic patois is much, much worse. Still, it would probably help sometimes if we didn't always keep everything to ourselves.

Shit, who knows? Maybe one day far, far, away, with intense schooling, re-education camps, and a hand from

---

[45] Most men (myself included) are complete nincompoops when it comes to ending romantic relationships. While we've invented myriad ways to completely fuck this process up, our course of action usually falls under one of the following categories:

1. "Stealth Bomber" What happens when we give absolutely no inkling that we're unhappy...until we actually tell her, "Yo, I'm unhappy. This shit aint gonna work," and bounce.
2. "The David Blaine" When we disappear off the face of the earth.
3. "The Sabotage" When we intentionally do fucked up shit just so they'll break up with us. While this level of break-up incompetence is inexcusable, I don't think women understand how difficult it is for a man to reject a woman. To analogize, it's like what would happen if you tried to domesticate a tiger. It's so used to being the hunter that it can't fully grasp living any other way, and eventually it's just going to say "fuck it" and bite your face off. –T.C.

evolution, women might even actually learn how to listen.

Friend-Zoned
6 Signs That You've Been Given the "Just a Friend" Title

By The Champ

"...I love talkin' bout your ex all night/we can stay up all night listening to your life...

...my, my, my, my, you're making me crazy, and....I don't know what you wanna do"

—From "The Friends Zone"—88 keys (featuring Shitake Monkey), a track from Keys's album "The Death of Adam"

It was 1991. Her name was Shatima, and she was the biracial (Black and Chinese) object of the 12 year old Champ's desire. Every day that summer, we'd play *Double Dribble* on Nintendo in her basement, and she'd bring me a glass of terrible lemonade from her kitchen. I was convinced she was my girlfriend, despite the fact that we hadn't actually hugged or kissed or even held hands. I guess the summertime heat fried my brain so much that it allowed me to conveniently forget the fact that she was 14 and about to enter high school, which made snotty-nosed 12 year old boys with baseless voices about as obsolete as a BETA tape.

This all changed one day towards the end of the summer, when her usually sunny disposition had disappeared. When I asked what was wrong, she replied...

127

"Alex doesn't wanna go with me anymore! Champ, you're a boy...help me. What should I do to get him to like me again???"

Instead of actually attempting to reply with the giant lump in my throat, I dropped the joystick, left, and never spoke to her again. I also refused to eat Chinese food for 5 years. Looking back, I had definitely been placed in the **"Friend Zone,"** and to ensure that *Shatima* doesn't happen to any guy ever again, here are **six signs that you've somehow fallen into that dreaded, coitus-less abyss.**

1. You're "dating," and she makes any reference whatsoever to anybody else she might be seeing. Even if it's unintentional (*which it never is*), most women aren't going to let a guy she's interested in know she's seeing other people, for fear it might scare him away.

Sure, there are women who'll say stuff like that just to hopefully make the guy she's interested in jealous, but that usually only occurs after a woman has already been Close-Bused and (wrongly) thinks this is the only way to get the guy more into her, not on the first or second date. Shit, she might be dating the entire roster of the Washington Wizards, but he'll never know. (Unless, of course, his cousin plays for the Wizards).

She might imply that she's *busy,* but if she's really into a cat, it stays the ambiguous *busy* instead of the ball-shrinkingly unambiguous *"Damn...do you realize this is my second date this week?? You're lucky you caught me."*

2. You all haven't been physical yet, but she makes any reference whatsoever to sex she's had before. Basically, if you're sitting around shooting the shit and she's telling you about that time a couple years ago in the movie theater, with the bus driver, the basketball trophy, and the stopwatch, consider yourself neutered. Most women aren't going to make blatant pronouncements about her past sexual deeds to a guy she thinks of as a potential romantic partner, unless those deeds are mentioned in a *"this is what I'm going to do to you later tonight"* context.

Again, this goes back to the "don't want to scare the guy away" concept because most women know that the easiest and surest way to scare a guy off is to introduce the concept of her having sex with another man in his head. Even though we assume each woman we meet past a certain age has been sexually active, most men will do everything they can to block that idea out of their heads.[46] Women are aware of this, and her freeness of the tongue is proof that she now officially looks at you as a *friend*, not a *potential sex partner*.

The next time you see her, you might as well just leave your balls in your glove compartment. If you're not going to use them, they should at least be somewhere safe.

---

[46] Why? While the common theory is that men typically don't want to be with someone who's been "around" because it implies that she's not a suitable prize ("What's the point of winning something everybody has already had?"), it goes a bit deeper than that. You see, men are extremely neurotic when thinking about our ability to sexually please and satisfy a woman we're with. In many of our minds, if she's been with enough people to fill the Carrier Dome, it would be virtually impossible to please her. What can you do for a woman who has already had everything done to them by everyone else? –*T.C.*

3. You go over to her place for the first time, and her apartment looks like hurricane Katrina just visited and she looks like she just completed a decathlon. As neurotic about appearances as most women are, there's no way in hell she's going to allow a guy she's actually interested to see her or her apartment at its *"worst"* before they actually sleep together. This is especially true with black women, who'd sooner die than let a guy she's seeing visit her place for the first time if said place hasn't been scrubbed, vacuumed, and incensed to the point that you'd think you were at a Westin in Harlem. Along with *"Soak it before you fry it"* and *"Always bet on Black,"* Big Momma also told them that *"No good man would want to be with a woman with a nasty-ass apartment,"* and they've lived by that tenet. Her not caring about how you perceive her place or her person means that you don't make her the least bit self-conscious, and the fact that you haven't made her the least bit self-conscious means that she doesn't ever want you anywhere near her ovaries.

4. Any compliment about her looks or her potential as a mate is responded to with the same lazy "thanks" you'd get after loaning a co-worker a broken pencil. Most women are aware if a guy is harboring unrequited romantic feelings for her. Since this can be a delicate subject, many might not just come out and say, *"Hey, I'm really, really not into you like that. At all,"* but they'll usually try to quickly diffuse any conversation that is leading to any type of romantic talk or feeling. Plus, they need to be nice to get as much mileage out of the free dinner and movies card as possible. **To expound:**

Guy complimenting *interested* woman: ***"Wow. You look great. You're really killing that dress tonight."***

Interested reply, accompanied with eye contact, a smile, a slight blush, and an undetectable tingle of the vagina: *"Thanks."*

She probably won't return the compliment immediately because she doesn't want to seem thirsty or desperate, but rest assured, she'll make at least one positive remark about his cologne, his demeanor, or the size and strength of his hands by the end of the night.

Guy complimenting *uninterested* woman: *"Wow. You look great. You're really killing that dress tonight."*

Uninterested reply, accompanied with a forced and somewhat condescending return compliment, to ease the awkwardness she's feeling: *"Awwww, thanks hun. Your socks are really nice too. They really compliment your knuckles."*

5. She either refers to you by one of the killer B's (*"Buddy"* or *"Brother"*) or uses this phrase (*"he's like a **fill in the blank** to me"*) at any time when describing you. Basically, anytime a woman doesn't use your name or an inside pet nickname she's given you when addressing you (i.e. *"Hey friend"* or *"I missed you, Pal"* instead of *"Hey Champ"* or *"Hey Rocky Balboa"*) or uses a simile when referring to you (*"You're like a great science teacher to me"*), rest assured that there won't be any SexyTime between you two in the near future. Seriously, just the thought of hearing this from a woman I'm interested in gives me cold sweats and hot flashes. I think I'm just going to move on.

6. She tells you she's not interested in or ready to be in a relationship...which is her polite way of saying she's not

interested in or ready to be in a relationship with
YOU...and she probably never will be.

If a woman actually says these words to you, **believe her.**
It's the realest thing she'll ever say.

Close-Bus Syndrome
Yup, Ladies. Guys Can Put You in the "Friends Zone"

By The Champ and Panama Jackson

It's common knowledge that women happily and freely employ the "Friend Zone," the infamous **coitus-less abyss where they take pleasure in turning unsuspecting men into eunuchs.** Intentionally turning their vaginas into wet blankets, they use this tactic to vet and hopefully discourage uninspiring and uninteresting potential mates. In fact, we even devoted an entire chapter to it. Go back and read it again if you have time.

What's not so common knowledge is the fact that...

...we do it too.

Please re-read this last sentence for ultimate clarity and resonance. Done yet? Okay

Yup, despite whatever you think about men being hound dogs who will sleep with anything with a pulse, men place women in the friend's zone all of the time. Thing is, while there's one easily perceptible tell to see if a guy's been friend zoned (*"Are they fucking?"*), the signs of a woman being friend zoned are much more subtle, mainly because a *man can sleep with and even be in a relationship with a woman he's placed there.*[47]

---

[47] I guess this sentence—*"...because a man can sleep with..."*—kind of contradicts the whole "Men aren't really hound dogs with indiscriminating dicks. We actually care about people and shit, too" theme from the first

133

What makes the male and the female friend zone similar is that in each case, the "Zoner" isn't giving the Friend what the Friend truly desires, while simultaneously getting exactly what they need from the Friend at that moment. A woman who places guys there gets the perks of a relationship (*friendship, companionship, etc*) without giving what the man really wants (*sex*). On the other hand, guys who place women there get the perks of a relationship (*sex, companionship*) without ever giving the woman what she really wants (*a long-term commitment and a strong emotional and spiritual connection*).

We've coined this phenomenon **"Close Bus Syndrome."** Why **Close Bus Syndrome**?

Well, it describes what happens when you're waiting for a city transit bus for a while, and the bus is late. Eventually you get tired of waiting for it, so you just end up catching a bus that might deliver you somewhere close to your destination. Instead of waiting on the bus you really want, you decide to take the close bus because it's raining outside and you're tired of standing and it's been a long day and you want to ride something, anything. When women have been friend zoned, they represent the **close buses**; being taken for **rides** by men who don't even sit down during the trip because they're bracing themselves to jump off at any moment.

It's not so much that he's just not that into you. He probably thinks you're attractive and worthy of a serious relationship. He's just not that into you *enough,* and he's using you as a placeholder until his situation changes or

---

sentence in this paragraph, doesn't it? Actually, you know what? Never mind. Don't answer that question. –*T.C.*

something better comes along. 9 times of out 10, it's the latter.

Anyway, just knowing why this occurs isn't enough. With this in mind, we've decided to share 10 signs that you might be a victim of **Close Bus Syndrome.**

1. You only see him when he's ***fill in the blank***. *Drunk. Tired. Horny. Sleepy. Hungry. Broke. Dopey. Sneezy. Bashful.*

Basically, if the adjective that fills in the blank sounds like it could be the name of one of the seven dwarfs, you've officially been close-bused. If a man only spends time with you under certain conditions (*i.e.: at night, after the club, on the weekend, etc*), and this is a consistent pattern, you might be seriously involved with him, but trust me, he definitely ain't seriously involved with you. If you were a meal, you'd be Stouffers French Bread Pizza instead of Sunday dinner at Big Momma's.

2. You always initiate all of the daytime contact. If every time you text or call, they say, *"I was just about to call you,"* they're lying. The law of averages teaches us this is wrong. If somebody's really invested in you, they're going to beat you to the punch at least a few times. This is especially true with the text message. At some point in every real relationship, you should be the recipient of the random 3pm, *"just thinking of you"* text, or even the *"I know you're at work, but I just wanted to say hello even if I* *couldn't hear your voice because I figured you could use a pick me up, lol :)"* text.[48]

If you never get the LOL :) …you're probably been close-bused.

3. You've never met any of his friends. You haven't even met his neighbors, co-workers, pets, or favorite Panera Bread waiter. In fact, you're not even fully convinced that you're not the only person on the planet who knows that this dude exists.

You see, guys like to show off women they're interested in and in relationships with, for two reasons:

A) This is our way of saying *"Guess who I bagged? And yup, I'm definitely hittin' that too! Jealous, ain't you?"* **to the rest of the world.** Guys are always competing with and looking for ways to one up each other, and showing off their women is one of our most

---

[48] Regularly calling and texting you during the day for absolutely no reason is definitely one of those super annoying *and* endearing things that women *only* do if they're truly into you. Every guy reading this has seen this scenario play out at least 317 times:

Her: *"Hey."*
Him: *"What's going on?"*
Her: *"Nothing much. Just sitting here at work, thinking about wallpaper, appliances, and Jews. Oh wait, did I tell you that I walked past like five mailboxes today??? Five!!! In one day. Can you believe that?"*
Him: *"That's crazy"*
Her: *"I know right? I think that broke my all-time record. Oh, I almost forgot: I called to tell you that I just found that pencil I was looking for last weekend. Don't you know it was in the pocket of my peacoat the entire time?"*
Him: *"Word?"*
Her: *"Yeah. Well, anyway honey, I gotta get back to work. I'll call you back in about seven or eight minutes." –T.C.*

common ways to get this done. This doesn't mean that we just want you to be trophy showpieces and Stepford wives. But, just as there's a problem if he only wants you around so he can show you off, it also means trouble for you if he never, ever does it.

B) To vet. If we're really into a woman, we'll let her meet the people close to us so they can offer their feelings about her to us. Although we trust our own judgment, we usually still like to get a second or seventh opinion about your qualities if we're seriously thinking about making things permanent with you.

If you've been seeing a guy for a decent amount of time, and you still haven't met *any* of his people, he's either hiding you because he thinks he'd catch a bestiality charge if people knew you were sleeping together, or he figures that you're not important enough to vet because you'll be gone soon anyway.

4. Not only is he seemingly never happy to see you (unless it involves sex), he never makes plans to spend "extra" time together. Basically, if he makes a face like an infant with gas every time he sees you or you attempt to discuss plans, I wouldn't start picking out the names of those grandchildren yet.

Also, by extra plans we mean, sure, he spends the bare minimum amount of quality time with you, but he never plans to do anything *extra*. He never invites you to do stuff together (i.e.: shopping, eating dinner, watching Netflix) that you could just as easily do apart.

You know somebody likes you when they find odd reasons to hang around you. If you always want just 5

137

more minutes of his time but he never wants to stay around, you're more jumpoff[49] than girlfriend. Even if it's just 8pm and he's like, *"It's getting late"*...yeah, no. You're a Close Bus.

5. He speaks to you with the exact same voice inflection and tone he uses when playing Madden with his boys. Even if its subconscious, most guys will change their tone and speech patterns a bit when speaking to a woman they're interested in, even if it's changing *niggas* to *nigras* or dropping the F-bomb once every 50 words instead of once every 10. This is especially true with phone conversations. For whatever reason, the phone makes our voices drop two octaves if we're talking to a woman we're interested in, and even Alvin from the Chipmunks will do his best Barry White impression if he's talking to a woman he really likes.

If you're his Close Bus, not only will you probably never get the *drop*, you're probably his nigga too. Not in the awww-inducing *"She's my road dawg, man. She's truly my*

---

[49] The jump-off/f-buddy is a between relationship staple of many 18 to 35 year olds, a stop-gap to momentarily fill a sexual void, the human version of Domino's Pizza delivery. Here are three things to remember if you don't want to fuck it up.

1. **No overnight stays.** I don't care if there's an F5 tornado mixed with a hurricane and gale-force typhoon winds outside. If you can't drive home, sleep in your car and pray that it isn't your time to go. Staying the night sends the wrong message. It says that you actually don't mind waking up to them in the morning, when truth is, you don't even want to see them after you finish going for the gold.

2. **No unnecessary conversations.** I strongly discourage this. In fact, I think that you shouldn't spend anymore than 30 minutes of time in each others presence fully clothed.

3. **No gifts.** To quote the great Joe Budden, "My jump off never has me going out of my way/And she don't want nothing on Valentine's Day." –PJ

nigga" sense, though, but in the "*Nigga, go make me some grits, nigga!*" sense.

6. You always get them thoughtful gifts, but he never seems to get you anything. Although someone buying you gifts isn't a concrete indicator that they're definitely into you, if a guy is able to spend but, for whatever reason, is never willing, you're probably being close-bused. Also, when men who've close-bused women do buy gifts, they're usually impersonal items he probably picked up at "Bullshit Relationships R Us."[50]

7. He always seems to be "on the way over." He was supposed to meet you out for dinner at 6:00 pm. It's 6:15 pm. You call him to find out where he is and he's "on the way over."

He was supposed to give you a ride to work this morning. You need to be there by 8:30 am. It's 8:25 am. You call to find out where he is and he's "on the way over."

It's 2:15 am, Saturday night. You're in bed, sleeping. You haven't heard from him all day. The phone rings, waking you up. It's him. He tells you that he's "on the way over."

It's 11:45am, Saturday morning. You're at the alter, waiting. You haven't heard from him all day. The pastor

---

[50] My personal favorite bullshit gift for a bullshit relationship is when a significant other leaves town on a vacation or business meeting, and returns with a plastic or wooden spoon with the name of the city or country they've visited written on the handle. Not only does that gift say "*I haven't really put any thought into you, whatsoever*", it also says "*In fact, I put so little thought into you that I didn't even remember I even had a girlfriend until I walked past the gift shop in the airport on the way back home*" –P.J.

calls him. He tells the wedding party that he's "on the way over." (Yes, married women can get close-bused too.)

8. You suggest interesting dates and end up at TGIFridays ...every time. Variety is the spice of life and shit. Well, let's rephrase that. Restaurant variety is the spice of many women's lives. While most men are cool with rotating the same three restaurants—especially if said restaurants have pictures of food on the menus—women seem to be more into shit like ambience and atmosphere.

There are many reasons for this, but the most relevant one is they figure if a guy is willing to take them there instead of the Burger King drive-thru, it's a sign that he cares somewhat about her wants. And, you know what....*she's right.*

Guys who close-bus women usually don't put that much thought into outings because, well, they haven't put that much thought into them. If you're always up for something new and different but you *always* end up at Outback Steak House, well, you're probably being close-bused. If he really cared about your happiness, you'd be at Benihana. But, you're not. If fact, because he's been "on the way over" for 45 minutes and you're waiting for him to meet you before you start to eat, your double-stack Baconator and fries are getting cold.

9. You were a consolation prize. If a man makes a serious *"there's no doubt in anyone's mind that I'm interested in this chick"* play for one of your girls, sisters, cousins, co-workers, parole officers, etc...**and gets thoroughly and publicly rejected,** there's no way in hell he's going to ever look at you as anything but a consolation prize, and consolations prizes get close-bused. If he was seriously into you, you have probably been the first person he approached, and he definitely wouldn't have had the balls to try and deal with you after everyone and they momma knows that you weren't his first choice.

Knowing this actually helps me understand why savvier women consider a man to be off-limits forever once one of their friends has dated him. He's definitely a passenger they won't be picking up.

10. He doesn't care about anything you do. Although we love to feign nonchalance about your mundane dailies because it makes us seem cool (and cool men get laid), we do actually care about the shit that women do...*if we care about them.*

We do really care about your new promotion, your new 'do, and even the little bullshit gossip going on within your crew because it all affects you. And, if we're truly into you, we care about what's affecting you.

Obviously, we care because your state-of-mind affects the relationship. But also, if we genuinely want to be with you, we genuinely *like* you as well. You're our homeskillet as well as our lover and partner, and what happens to you matters to us because we want our homeskillets to be happy.

If we don't really care?

Let's just say that if *"I'm moving next week,"* *"I think I'm gonna cut my hair like Tong Po in Kickboxer,"* and *"I think I lost my citizenship"* are all met with the same lazy shrug and half-hearted *"Damn...that's messed up"* as he

141

looks up from his carpet and continues playing solitaire on his phone, maybe it's time to re-think those joint lease plans.

Diva Dudes, Kryptonite Chicks, and Crazy Bastards
The Relationship Jabberwockies

By The Champ

In the 2005 sweaty masterpiece *Hustle & Flow*, Terrence Howard's "DJay"—a Memphis area pimp— rapped that *"It's hard out here for a pimp."* While neither Panama nor I can confirm or deny the validity of this pimping related angst, we decided to write this book because we can both definitely attest to the fact that it's hard out here for a dater.

And, while there are certain types of people who are so faulty that even Stevie Wonder can see them coming, there are more than a few excessively faulty types whose StayTheFuckAwayFromThem-ness is stealth; abstruse assholes with clandestine but cavernous chips in their relationship armor. **The Diva Dude, The Kryptonite Chick, and The Crazy Bastard** are three such types.

Let me expound.

An epidemic unique to the black community, the **"Diva Dude"** describes the mindset created in certain black men, developed after reading and hearing about the *shortage of good black men* that's supposedly sweeping through the country at a pandemic rate. It's a condition, an aura which basically lets every eligible woman within a 25 mile radius know *"Look, I've read the same articles that you have, and since I'm such an 'endangered species,' I pretty much have carte blanche to do whatever the hell I want with you. Kiss the ring, desperate bitch."*

143

There are Diva Dudes walking among us, twirling blue and white sticks and passive-aggressively suggesting Dutch first dates as we speak, and it's one of our crime-fighting duties to locate and brand them before they continue to poison the already murky dating pool.

Here are a few characteristics and behaviors synonymous of the Diva Dude. If any man possesses seven or more of these traits, he qualifies. Think of this as a Dating DSM-IV.[51]

1. They're straight and single with no kids, 21 to 35 years old with advanced degrees and decent jobs, cars, and apartments/condos. Basically, they're the remaining 7.2% left out when ABC's "Nightline" does their annual feature about black relationships; a story that will definitely include at least one hysterical *"92.8% of black men are either dead, in jail, unemployable, still rocking FUBU, or sleeping with a Kardashian"* graphic.

2. They live in college towns or cities with metropolitan areas over 500,000 people. This is very important, for two reasons:

A) If they're living in a large metropolitan area, there are probably *at least* 1.5 times more eligible women than men (or, at least, the **perception** that women vastly

---

[51] I want to make it clear that being a young and successful black man definitely doesn't automatically make you a Diva Dude. Diva Dudes are bred in insecurity; grown-ass babies who need a woman's attention to validate their existence. Basically, these are the type of cats who would all of a sudden start using initials for their first names when becoming successful, thinking that "T. Jonathan Butler" on a business card might procure more panties than regular ol' "Tyrone J. Butler" ever did. –*T.C.*

outnumber the men). This fact allows the Diva Dude to basically get away with their bullshit unfettered.

B) If a group of women get wise and catches them, recognizing in them numerous Diva Dude characteristics, there's always another mall or happy hour or convention somewhere in the city where the *mythical eligible black man* shtick will guarantee free panties. There are suckers for DDs with degrees born every minute.

3. They've been the proverbial ugly duckling until very recently. This is important, because the fact that they weren't getting any rhythm before they became notable creates an inherent bitchassedness that permeates everything they do. From what I understand, this seems to be pretty common with black male Greeks.[52]

4. They're only friends with other diva dudes. All DDs are close friends with between one and four other diva dudes, a safe number which gives them a couple clubbing and drinking buddies, but not so many that their diva light doesn't shine as bright. Remember, these are not alphas dogs, just a bunch of beta dicks constantly thirsty for attention. Basically, this is the type of guy whose dick would get harder at the thought of a chick at the mall double-taking while he's walking past her and jigging Audi keys in his hand than it would if he actually slept with her.

---

[52] As you've probably noticed, this book has a few matter-of-fact shots at the black Greek population. This is intentional. We love the black fraternities and sororities, but we love picking with and poking them even more. Trust me, you haven't lived until you make a snide remark on your blog about Alphas, and then receive a 3000 word email the next day from a pissed off guy with waaaay too many names (i.e.: *"James Robert Joseph Jackson Jenkins III, Esquire"*) demanding an apology for besmirching his and Martin Luther King Jr.'s names. *–T.C.*

145

5. They're not chivalrous and proud of it. There's nothing that screams *"I'm a Diva Dude"* louder than a grown ass man who's practically excited to get the opportunity to let everyone else know all the simple shit *he'd never do* for a woman.

"Pay for dinner? Trick, please. What I look like buying you appetizers and water and shit when you don't even swallow? Plus, you make like 31g's a year! You're telling me you can't afford to buy your own damn iced tea?"

Part of being a grown-ass man is doing the right thing without any expectation of acknowledgment or reward, but a typical DD will voluntarily and happily relinquish a crucial component of his own manhood just because some janky broad or two didn't immediately fellate him when he gave up his seat for her on the train seven years ago.

6. They LOVE to scapegoat. Diva Dudes love blanket statements, scapegoating and pigeonholing more than crackheads love Home Depot. Words such as *all* and *every* always seem to find a way into their sentences when speaking negatively about the opposite sex, a common practice used by folks so blinded by bitterness that they can't see how foolish a statement such as, *"All black women with Master's degrees give terrible blow jobs,"* really is.

7. They're delusional. There's nothing a DD loathes more than actually admitting that he's a DD, a phenomenon which produces some of the most hilariously misguided attempts of synonym use known to man. From *practical* and *prudent* to *rational* and *realistic,* a typical DD will have an endless supply of words and euphemisms that make his DIVA-ness sound much less harsh.

"I'm not bitter. Far from it. I just tend to look at the entire idea of womankind in a perpetually jaundiced light, that's all."

8. They're in a ton of fucking party pictures. Seriously, if you're ever at a mixer or happy hour somewhere and you're looking for a Diva Dude or three, just find the ridiculously overdressed cats faux ice-grilling a camera while clutching Mojitos.

9. They don't actually date. Instead of actual dates, Diva Dudes only interact with women they're interested in through **meet-ups**—courting arrangements specifically designed to alibi them out of any real expectation or accountability.

Saying shit like *"Let's chill together sometime soon"* instead of *"Friday, I'm gonna take U to da movies"*[53] is an affected verbal manipulation allowing them to reap the benefits of a commitment without actually committing to anything. There's a reason God hates lawyers.

Admittedly, there is a certain allure to living this lifestyle. Not so much in the DD actions, but in the figurative thumbing of the nose at all the shit saying that all black men between 21 and 35 are either imprisoned, uneducated, unemployed, or gay. But, despite the attraction to this state of mind, you have to remember that these are the dudes who probably will end

---

[53] Word to **Bangs**, the Very Smart Brothas' favorite Sudanese rap icon. – *T.C.*

up like Champ Kind from Anchorman when they reach 40; single, lonely, and unable to function without the aid of his crew of like-minded relationship nincompoops. Destined to a lifetime of terribly furnished apartments and occasionally getting lucky when some 19 year old working the hot dog stand in front of the club is impressed with his red corvette.

While the **Diva Dude** does his damage in the daytime, the **Kryptonite Chick** does her deeds in the dark recesses of the male mind. Basically, we think she's hot, so we put up with stuff we probably should not.

Swayed by a great smile, a perfect body, or amazing sex, sometimes we have a tendency to stay involved with poisonous women, so entranced by the view at the beach that we fail to realize all of the fish are dead. We ignore the signs and don't heed the warnings, and end up surprised when that super cute hammerhead shark bites our forearm off.

While there are many types of **Kryptonite Chicks**, there seems to be 11 that men seem to repeatedly fall victim to. Hopefully those of us lusting over them will stop daydreaming about their impressive boobage long enough to listen, leaving us more time to find some Very Smart women to date and mate with.

1. Ms. "My Friends Ain't Shit" "Ain't shit" chicks run in packs, like wild wolves or jaded liberals. Basically, if at least half of her girlfriends could have easily auditioned for a part on a VH1 reality show, delete her number as soon as possible. If that doesn't work, just leave the country.

2. Ms. Outrageous Ultimatums (MOUS) What makes MOUS-es so dangerous is the fact that they have no problem with simultaneously utilizing two of the most difficult tactics for a man to deal with: **The Guilt Trip** (*every mother reading this is nodding her head in silent affirmation*) and **The Threat** (*most men have no idea how to respond to threats when physical violence isn't an option*).

Influenced by an ass-to-waist ratio rivaling a circa *Selena*-era Jennifer Lopez, I once let a **MOUS** strong arm me into ending a relationship with a close college friend I *hadn't even seen* in four years, just because the MOUS found out that we had been intimate a few times almost a decade earlier. The friend and I haven't spoken since. The **MOUS?** Three words: Eventual restraining order.

3. Ms. 0 to 60 in Less Than 3 Seconds. Being conditioned to accept that women are highly emotional and irrational beings has led many of us to excuse clearly bipolar behavior under the guise of *"She's a woman. It's okay."* Nevermind the time when you were three minutes late for picking her up from work and she stabbed you in the shoulder with a nail file, or the time you told her she looked nice and she bawled uncontrollably for 17 consecutive minutes until she fainted. She's a woman, so it's okay.

4. Ms. "I Suck at Life" I'll admit, there's a certain allure in dealing with Lemony Snickets, women whose lives are a continual series of unfortunate events. These women give you the opportunity to play Ironman or Dr. Manhattan while letting your dramaless-ness be an aphrodisiac. There's a reason women whose lives are a mess are usually great in bed. Still, eventually the trials and tribulations of her life will affect you, and each of your days will become a scene from *Final Destination 3*; you unsuccessfully trying to avoid the ever approaching deathgrip of shittyness that is her life.

5. Ms. "You Know, I Usually Don't Date Guys Like You. You Must Have Caught Me On an Off Day or Something" There's a reason for that. The rest of the *guys like you* were smart enough to run the fuck away when they saw her coming.

6. Ms. Pretentious For clarity, African-American Ms. Pretentious-es usually share each of the following traits:

A) They refuse to eat at chain restaurants. I don't know what's worse, the fact that people actually think like this, or the fact that people think like this and actually aren't ashamed to admit it in public.

B) They've often referred to themselves as "The black... " *(i.e.: "the black Carrie Bradshaw," "the black Kimora Lee Simmons," "the black Verne Troyer" etc).*

C) They continually brag about their eclectic tastes. You have Joni Mitchell, Janis Joplin, and G-Unit in your iPod? Whoopdy fucking gotdamn doo. Do you want a sugar cookie? Fine. Now take it and shove it up your ass.

7. Ms. "You'll Have to Pry My Mouth Open With the Jaws of Life If You Want Me to Smile" Women with serious mental and/or emotional issues are excused from the whole never smiling thing. Thing is, if they're not clinically depressed and they still haven't cracked a smile in public since Eriq Lasalle was still on "ER," maybe it's time to accidentally forget to restore her number the next time your Blackberry Storm breaks.

Also, smiling is sexy. Very, very sexy. Seriously, I've had a crush on Jill Scott for almost a decade now just because of her smile and the possibility that she'd make me early morning fish and grits while smiling that sexy ass smile.

8. Ms. "I Don't Really Get Along With Other Women"
This statement is usually code for either "*I don't really get along with other women because I'm a backstabbing bitch who tried to steal each of their boyfriends*" or "*Because I don't have any friends, I'm going to expect you to be my sole source of entertainment for the duration of the relationship.*"

9. Ms. Super-Sexy Hoodrat.[54] She's tempting because her uber sexiness (and fighting ability) is enough to almost make you forget that the man whose initials are tattooed on her ass cheeks murdered your neighbor two years ago. But, she becomes toxic once you realize your life expectancy decreases by 5% every week you're together. Plus, it doesn't help that her teenage son can (and will, if prompted) whoop your ass.

---

[54] Although "Hoodrat" and "Hood chick" sound similar, they're completely different terms with different connotations. There's nothing wrong with being a hood chick, as it implies that you probably have an uncommon level of resourcefulness, character, and loyal to a fault-ness. On the other hand, you can be a hoodrat—an excessively ignorant and scandalous scalawag—without actually being from the hood. If this doesn't make any sense, just watch an episode of "Basketball Wives" and you'll understand.—*T.C.*

10. Ms. "Think Like a Man...and Act Like a Man Too"
You've been complaining all your life about women and
their emotional instability, so you rejoice when you
finally meet a chick who is ultra assertive, rational,
practical, and actually kicks *you* out of bed (and her crib)
after sex.

But, between the embarrassment you'll feel during sex
when you say *"Whose is it??"* and she replies *"Not yours,
weak dick muthafucker,"* the annoyance you'll feel when
you realize she hasn't *listened* to a single word you've
said since January 2009, and the fact that her general
blasé attitude about intimacy makes you (rightly)
suspect that she's slept with at least 150 guys, she's not
worth the trouble.

Plus, when you break up, she'll probably start dating
before you do, and her new guy will probably be an
upgrade.

**11. Ms. Much, Much Younger Than Me (aka Ms.
Tenderoni)** At first glance, most Tenderonis are perfect.
No cellulite, no kids, no real baggage, no non-perkiness
anywhere, no real income (*which, combined with your age,
means you'd probably wield complete relationship power*), no
world-weary cynicism (*which means she'll believe
everything you say*), and no qualms about entering *and
winning* the "How Low Can You Go" contest at the club
for two Mos Def tickets (*you always wanted to see him
live*). And, to be perfectly honest, she's not really toxic.

But, you'll eventually tire of teaching her how to cook
and telling her why it's not appropriate to send work
emails in tweet speak. Also, although you might have
frequent sex, since we've already established that most

women don't actually get good in bed until they're 25, you'll probably tire of that too.

Lastly, there's a type that affects both genders; a person who seems perfectly fine, until a circumstance or two reveals that you've allowed a **Crazy Bastard**—a relationship terrorist holding you and your sanity hostage—into your life, and here are a few signs to help you know when you should probably go into the Anonymous Relationship Protection Program.

1. You're scared to break up...for two separate reasons:

A) What they'll potentially do to you.

B) What they'll potentially do to themselves.

"How did it last that long?"

Ask anybody who's stayed in a relationship with a slightly anti-sane person this question, and they'll all give you a variant of the same answer.

"Yeah, of course. I was deathly afraid she'd delete my hard drive and steal all of my television remotes if I ended it. But, to be honest, I was more scared about what she'd do to herself. Shit. Suicide, homicide, deer murder...anything was possible."

2. You keep a list in your head of completely and hilariously random topics you try to never, ever, ever, ever bring up. Several years ago, I dated a woman who'd go batshit whenever anything having to do with vegetables was brought up. I'm not making this up. Vegetables!!!!

153

Do you realize how often you have to play on a verbal landmine during the course of the day to make sure you don't mention or do anything that reminds a person of a vegetable? She was hot so I put up with it initially, but due to the slight stutter I was developing because of all the times I had to bite my own tongue, I had to end it after a couple of months.[55]

Moral of the story? *Don't date Deltas.*

3. They have a list of completely and hilariously random places they're never, ever, ever allowed visiting anymore. Chuck E. Cheese. Wal-Mart. Back yards. Madison Square Garden. Bridges. The state of Delaware. Within 500 yards of any post office or beer distributors.

No matter how stupid the reason, crazy-ass bastards love being banned from random ass, seemingly unbanable places. It's a virtual rite of passage for them, like confirmation for Catholics or a sex-tape for a socialite. Thing is, sometimes it's just them being paranoid. And, *sometimes they're right.* Sometimes they've actually caused so much havoc somewhere that the establishment posted a picture of them on its door and its website with explicit instructions to call the National Guard or Michelle Obama if that face ever walks into its doors again.

4. They've been subtly stalking you. A common theme with dating a crazy bastard is that they always seem to know a little bit more about you than they actually should, and this is usually done through subtle stalking.

---

[55] Actually, this is a lie. She was too good-looking for me to end it that soon, and I probably wouldn't have if she didn't join that gotdamn cult. *—T.C.*

I'm not referring to criminal level or even garden-variety Lifetime movie starring Jennifer Jason Lee and Meredith Baxter-Birney type of stalking, but shit that makes you ask yourself, *"Wait. How did he know the name of my 8th grade math teacher? I don't think I ever told him that"* and *"I wonder why she keeps leaving comments on Facebook pictures I uploaded three years ago?"*

Also, Google is the subtle stalking crazy bastards best friend, so don't be surprised if you happen to get on their laptop and find your name and every possible relevant word combo (*i.e.: "Kim Jones BlackPlanet Profile"* or *"Kim Jones Pittsburgh Stripper"*) popping up in their recently searched items.

5. For whatever reason, sex is usually accompanied by tears. Or fighting. Or worse. Lets just say I learned the hard way that a woman doing a naked wall-slide and sobbingly uncontrollably for ten minutes directly after an orgasm *isn't* a good thing, and could possibly lead to more terrifyingly hilarious (or hilariously terrifying?) behavior, and lets just leave it at that, okay?

6. They've made you crazy too. Whether it's changing your account passwords twice a week, *hacking their email just to see if they've hacked yours,* or finding yourself apologizing for completely and utterly defensible shit— *"I'm sorry for telling you I got to work on time yesterday. I didn't realize it would make you think about the things your stepfather's foster kids used to do to you"*—there's no truer sign that you're dating a crazy bastard than the fact that **you've started to do crazy-ass shit yourself,** just to potentially preempt their gotdamn crazy bastard-ness.

This—*"there's no truer sign that you're dating a crazy bastard than the fact that you've started to do crazy-ass shit yourself"*—can actually be applied to each of the relationship jabberwockies. Their defectiveness can be extremely contagious, and this contagiousness can be very, very stealth. Shit, just three dates worth of listening to an especially exasperating **Diva Dude** bitch and moan about why black chicks from Great Britain are better than sistas from Baltimore can cause a *regular and drama-free black woman* to permanently morph into **Ms. Outrageous Ultimatums;** exactly why, to ensure you stay on the Very Smart path to dating and relationship proficiency, you need to take proper steps to avoid them.

Dating the 30 Year Old Virgin
A Very Smart Rant from Panama Jackson

Honestly, considering the rate of STDs flying around, it's actually not completely out of this world to think that dating a virgin is a good idea. If anything, at least you know you're not catching a chick with an ignited crotch-rocket from being the wick for too many firecrackers.

I should know. In my mid 20's I dated one for two years. Smartly, very few grown adult women state that *they'd* like to date a virgin. Apparently, women don't like being the teachers, which is more than a bit ironic since most schoolteachers are women...and sleeping with 15 year old boys.

Anyway, dating a virgin requires a lot of finesse. Let's face it; you're probably not getting any real lovin' during the duration of your duress unless you *"Put a ring on it."* But, since everyone's not Beyonce, here's a quick little guide for how to make sure you don't break from the pressure of your girlfriend's chastity belt.

1. Stock up on plenty of <u>Jergens</u> (preferably the scent-less options). If you're dating a woman who doesn't go all the way, you're probably going to spend more time choking your own chicken than you'll spend cooking any actual chicken. Unless, of course, you're probably messing with someone who *does everything but go all the way,* the cruel batter who leaves runners stranded at second base every inning. In this case, you'll probably have to choke your chicken to keep from choking her.

2. Get some very interesting hobbies. I'd probably suggest crocheting. You're already not sleeping with your girl, which makes you kind of lame, so you might as well be the lame dude who crochets too. Or knit. Both lame, but definitely time-consuming and productive.

3. Work out like crazy. You're going to have to release that raw energy somewhere. Nautilus seems like the best option because it gives you a quick and easy alternative if you're too sore from too much number 1.

4. Take some time to develop the inner, spiritual you. Face it, you're going to have a lot of time to reflect on who you are as a person now that you're not making the beast with two backs. You can read a ton of Chicken Soup books, pray to Buddha, and look for your own spiritual awakening, especially since you won't be awakening any morning wood anytime soon, Lumberjack.

5. Just don't date her. This is the safest option, especially since it's been proven that men need to have at least 3 orgasms a week to prevent us from going on mass murdering sprees. I mean really, why in Sam Hill would you do that to yourself anyway? Seems like a bad idea, unless, of course you actually want to spend time talking to her, learning about her feelings, building trust, and creating a genuine and comfortable foundation so she'll eventually be comfortable sharing her body with you.

Eh. Nevermind. That takes too much work. How much does a Nautilus machine cost again?

She Really Likes You
A Very Smart Rant from The Champ

Forget everything else you've seen. Disregard every other theory you've read. Ignore anything you've heard from any other relationship pundit. **Fellas, you need to know that** *it's all about money.*

It's not about *sex,* or, more specifically, which sexual acts she's willing to do for you. She swallowed? So what. Get in line. Take a number. You doo-scooped her in one of the men's dressing rooms at Banana Republic? Shit, so did Clinton Portis in 2002. Get over yourself.

It's not about *time* either. Many women will spend time with a guy they have no intentions on ever doing anything remotely physical with, sans the "church hug"—*the teasingly platonic hug where women hunch their backs forward and stick their behinds out, ensuring there won't be any type of crotch-area contact*—at the end of the night when you drop her off at her apartment.

She let you meet her girlfriends? Who cares? She just wanted to prove to them that she found someone worse in spades than she is. Plus, 45% of them aren't going to be around this time next year anyway.

She let you meet her family? So what? She's just tired of hearing the *"When are you getting married?"* chorus at every family outing, and figures that being seen with your delusional ass might buy her a good 6 months of question quelling.

She follows you on Twitter? Great. She also follows Wal-Mart. And, her grandmother.

159

She told you she loved you? Love schmove. When she said it she was probably under the influence of *DGP*— *"damn good pipe"*—and that "confession" definitely ain't admissible in any court. If you remember, that night she also called you *Bucketman* repeatedly, even though your name is Nate.

No, their only true tell, the one sign that'll make you absolutely certain that a woman is definitely, without any questions, *into you* is if she's willing to *give you money*.

Not borrow. Not loan. **Give.** Give with absolutely no plans to ever get it back. This is the ultimate test, the relationship Wonderlic exam. If she's willing, she adores you. If she's not, she doesn't. It's that simple.

I'm not suggesting that all women are bronze excavators (*gold-diggers* is a bit too clichéd for my taste), but let's just say that it's much, much, much easier to separate a man interested in a woman from miscellaneous cash than vice versa; and for her to be willing to actually do this for a guy she's seeing is the most concrete proof on the planet that she's invested in him.

From the moment they first learned how to say Lebron, most women are (rightly) taught that a man who isn't willing to be chivalrous or pay for dates probably isn't a man worthy of serious consideration.[56] When you combine this with the fact that the nightclub industry actually drives its business around unique ways for women not having to pay to party, you can understand

---

[56] **Extremely Naked (and extremely offensive) Dating Truth #92**: Truly smart women marry *up*, and do so unabashedly and unapologetically. Truly smart men find these truly smart women, blow their backs out, and send them back to their husbands, smiling and happy. *–T.C.*

why they might be a bit more reluctant than men are to finance their fun with the opposite sex in any way. Because of this, a woman typically has to be extremely into a guy to even consider giving him a portion of the hard-earned dough she saved from not having to pay for all of those drinks.

I'm also not saying that men need to go around asking their girlfriends for money to prove that she's truly into him, because that's one of the quickest ways to get your own page on girldontdatehisbrokeass.com. But believe me when I say that her *offering*—and the fake reach for the check on the second date doesn't count as offering— to do that is concrete proof that she's singing the *"Sittin in the Tree, K-I-S-S-I-N-G"* song in her head about you.

You could even make the argument that women put more value in their purses than their, *you know*. (*Think of a word that starts with "p" and rhymes with "gushies."*) You don't believe me? Okay. Tomorrow, ask each of the women in your sphere of influence how many people she's had any type of sexual relationship with.[57] Then, ask each of them how many of those guys they would have given $500 to if they needed it. I'd bet my Obama sponsored reparations check that at least 70% of the time, those numbers won't even be close to matching up.

Let's break it down again: *You met her stepmom?* So what? She *hates* her stepmom, and she just brought you around because she knows she'll be allergic to your cologne. She's actually secretly hoping that it kills her.

---

[57] Actually, don't do this, unless you plan on getting smacked repeatedly. Wait, on second thought, do this, record the results, and post them to YouTube under '*The Champ told me do to this"*. –T.C.

She let you make a tape? Hmmm...obviously you haven't checked the contents of that shoebox underneath her bed. You're just this month's co-star.

Your checking account is a bit short this month because you had to help pay for your aunt's funeral, and your girl gave you $550 to help out with your mortgage? She's already picked the names of your first three grandchildren.

Smiley Face
10 Sure-Fire Ways to Charm a Very Smart Man

By The Champ and Panama Jackson

Although it usually doesn't take much more than a nice ass-to-waist ratio to get us all verklempt and mushy on the inside, there are a few simple things a woman can do to exponentially improve her chances to go from *"She's nice. I think she'd make a great long-time sidepiece"* to *"She's nice. I wonder when Tiffany's is having a sale on engagement rings again."*

1. Know and be able to converse about hip-hop, and any other forms of music women stereotypically aren't supposed to be knowledgeable about. If you're dealing with a cat who's really into hip-hop, actual hip-hop knowledge will more than likely catch him off guard. You see, we expect women to know about other genres like pop or R&B/soul, but since hip-hop is such a male-dominated industry, meeting a woman who can go back and forth about the bars on the two bonus tracks off of the first "The Blueprint" genuinely intrigues us. Knowing that Lil Wayne exists is good, but Martians know who Lil Wayne is. But, if you can name the entire roster of the Wu-Tang Clan...well...damn. Pretty much every woman with even a passing knowledge of hip-hop knows who Method Man is, but I'd bet 3 out of 2,876 know who Masta Killa is (and that's including his momma and each of his baby-mommas).

We know it seems like we're stressing music a bit too much, but most men are closet music snobs who assume we know more about good music than everyone else (women especially), so being able to hold your own in this regard is like owning a Hemi engine while everyone else is on a 12-speed. With that in mind, we also relish a woman who can school us, or give us knowledge about a genre we know absolutely nothing about. Trust, women who can wax philosophical about Thelonius Monk's place in the jazz canon will almost always stand out, even if the dude has no clue what you're talking about.

2. Be a *quotable* movie buff. We're not talking about shit like *The Notebook* or the God awful *Twilight* flicks, but instead the ability to be able to go toe to toe with anybody on scenes from anything from *The Anchorman* to *The Godfather*. Seeing them is cool, but being able to quote them verbatim when necessary is nothing short of awesome. A well-timed pop culture movie quote from *Coming to America* will always draw positive attention to you, sexy lady. We promise. If you can fill out a dress *and* know when and where it's appropriate to belt out *"She's your Queeeeeeeeeeen to be…"* you'll have your man praying for God to grant you an extra left hand so he can put two rings on your fingers.[58]

---

[58] Bonus points if you can find a way to incorporate one of these quotes from *Coming to America* into your daily lexicon:

"Is it just me, or does every woman in New York have a severe emotional problem?"

"The royal penis is clean, your Highness." (Mostly because what man doesn't want to hear this? Even better if the one cleaning the royal peen is Garcelle Beauvais.)

"Hey, I started out mopping the floor just like you guys. But now… now I'm washing lettuce. Soon I'll be on fries; then the grill. And pretty soon, I'll make assistant manager, and that's when the big bucks start rolling in."

3. Let him "catch" you, ummm, you know (*to only be utilized if you're already sleeping with him*).

Scenario:

It's nighttime and you're both hanging out at his apartment. Since it's late and his crib is only a 10 minute drive from your job, you're spending the night. You've showered already, and you're just sitting there, messing around on the internet when he announces that he's going to hop in the shower real quick. Now, you already know that you're going to get some tonight. Shit, you're planning on it; that's the only reason why your ass is spending the night in his hot ass, no snacks sans for stale granola bars ass, apartment. You also know that the festivities will probably start soon after he gets out the shower and hops into bed. So, what do you do?

Start without him. Yup. You read it right. Start *poppin the Pepsi can* while his ass is still in the shower, so that when he exits the bathroom the first sight he sees is a woman so horny and so thirsty for it that she couldn't even wait for him to finish his 240 second rabbit shower. If he's already digging you, and you do shit like that on a semi-regular basis, I'm not saying he'll propose to you, or even suggest the thought of that to you aloud. But, best believe, he'll damned sure be thinking about ring sizes and payment plans the next time he walks past Zales in the mall.

4. Give him compliments, and say thanks every once in a while. It may not seem like a big deal, but little stuff like this lets us know that we're appreciated, and we

---

"His mamma call him Clay, imma call him Clay." –P.J.

appreciate knowing that we're appreciated. We're so used to being the compliment givers that you'd be surprised how far a small *"Thanks for picking me up from work the other day"* or a *"Those new shoes you bought are hot. Seriously, I'm impressed"* can go. Be careful, though. Because we're not used to hearing them, a man receiving a sincere compliment from a woman he's seeing is liable to immediately start crying or violently convulsing.

5. Wear his clothes whenever you have the opportunity to. We have absolutely no idea why, but it seriously does something to a man when a woman uses one of his old t-shirts as her night shirt or spends a lazy Saturday lounging around his place wearing nothing but one of his college sweatshirts. Our theory is that her eagerness to wear something that's undoubtedly his, a random and inglorious garment from his closet, shows a man that the woman has fully immersed herself in the idea of *Him*. Trust us when we say that there's nothing better than a night of monkey matrix sex followed by waking up to your chick making eggs and shit while she's rocking one of your summer league basketball shirts from 2002.

6. Have a sense of humor. Men generally feel the same way about humor that we do about music. In fact, you can even make the case that we're even snobbier about what is and isn't funny than we are about what constitutes good music. So, if a woman we're already into sends us a 6 word text message at work that makes us laugh uncontrollably for the next 30 minutes, she'll usually be placed in the keeper category.

If you've been cursed with the unfunny gene, at least have the ability to get jokes and recognize humor. You know he likes Bill Simmons, so email him a link to his latest podcast. Make your own version of The Aristocrat joke, and recite it to him. Even if it bombs terribly, he'll appreciate the effort, and give you unprompted cunnilingus to thank you for it.

With that being said, we'd be remiss if we didn't mention the fact that there is such a thing as a woman being *too* funny. And, the difference between *funny* and *too funny* is usually answered with one simple question: **Does she make sarcastic jokes about me around company?** While light-natured ribbing is great, hearing biting humor from your woman about your sore spots can be very emasculating, and emasculated men go on mass murdering sprees.

7. Create something. Do something that is completely unique to you two and your relationship. You could have bought that cologne for anyone, but that mix you made for him with all the unreleased Wu-Tang tracks from 1993 to 1998 is something based on his tastes that you knew he'd personally appreciate, and he'll definitely let you sleep in the dry spot for the rest of the month because of it.

8. Have standards without being pretentious. We bet a year's supply of KY that if you asked 100 happily married men to describe the best qualities of their wives, one of the first things out of most of their mouths will have something to do with *"she's really down to earth"* not *"she refuses to eat at a restaurant that has pictures on the menu."*

9. Put your foot in it. Look, you could look like the construction workers from *Fraggle Rock*, but if you can throw down in the bedroom *and the kitchen,* your man will do anything for you.

"Kick-slam my great-aunt? Sure baby. Just make sure you add that special seasoning to the gravy when I get back. I love you!!!"

We're almost certain that if you did a random poll of prisoners, asking them if their mate made them great breakfast on the morning they committed their crime, at least 85% of them would say "No"...and start sobbingly uncontrollably. Basically, great omelets equal happy men, and, well, you should know the rest by now.

10. Be Ray Allen. In the summer of 2007, perennial NBA all-star Ray Allen pushed to get traded from the Seattle Supersonics. Tired of balling in relative obscurity for a non-contending team, Allen wanted to be moved to a team with a better shot of winning, even if it meant sacrificing his own statistics. He landed with the Boston Celtics, and took a role on the team that saw his production drop almost 30%. Because of his self-inflicted personal decline, he was able to be a vital cog in the machine that won the 2008 NBA championship.

When men give the *"she'll make a great wife"* designation, there's a huge distinction between the Ray Allens of the world—stars willing to play a role if needed—and the Stephon Marburys of the world—wildly entertaining stars that you'll never, ever, ever go anywhere with. While the Marburys might use their unbelievable sex appeal to get extra onion rings to go with their chicken fingers, the Ray Allens usually get rings on their fingers.

Proving My Love
12 Extremely Painful Things Men Do Only Because They Love Women

By The Champ and Panama Jackson

Between wars, fantasy sports, and public farting, we recognize that women have to put up with a ton of nonsense at the hands of men. However, sometimes they don't really give us our due; failing to recognize the many dangerous, disgusting, and demeaning things we subject ourselves to just to make them happy.

1. Kill rodents. Nobody wants to see Mickey Mouse running around their house. Or Jerry. *(Wait, which one was the mouse again; Tom or Jerry? Never mind. They both sucked.)* However, we got them out of our houses, so why do we have to go to your house, risking life and limb to run down Fievel's second cousin? Isn't that why you all put men in the friend's zone, so you'll have somebody on call to come over and do shit like this? We come, though, because we love you. But word to Big Bird, if you have a beaver in your basement, call Ghostbusters, not VSB.

2. Kill scary-ass bugs. You know what, you're right. So what if we're asleep. You saw a cricket, and you don't want any crickets in your house, so we need to come kill it, pronto. Trekking across town at 2 am isn't that big a deal anyway. We're half awake, so there's only a 50% chance of us dying in a head-on collision with a tree as we try to avoid the beaver in the road that was hiding in your place because you wanted us to kill it instead of the Beaver Patrol.

But, we come over and kill the cricket because we love our women, and because it's funny seeing them scared to death of something 1/100,000 of their size.

3. Keep our phones on vibrate. See, a man's ringing phone is fodder for *"Who the fuck is that?"* And, unless it's someone related to us, the answer usually doesn't suffice. Because we're pissed that you're questioning our private property, you get pissed that we're pissed for you questioning us. It's a vicious cycle. Just be glad we're thinking of your sanity, ma'am!

4. Don't commit. Think about it: What's the best way to sharpen your debate skills? Deal with people who refuse to commit to a side or nail down an opinion. And, because so many men attempt to avoid commitment, women are forced to become better arguers and deciders, and this works wonders for diplomacy and world peace. Shit, after years arguing with her husband about the definition of *is*, is it any surprise that Hillary Clinton is such a great Secretary of State?

5. Allow you all to buy clothes for us that we'd never buy under any circumstance. We have our own clothes already, but women continue to add to our piles by buying us shit we hate, allowing us more opportunity to re-gift and donate to the Goodwill. It's a win-win for all, actually.

6. Just stay out until the next morning when we realize we happen to be out *too* late. We know this reasons seems a bit, um, retarded. But, if you think about it, this gives everybody time to come up with good reasons why he could possibly be out that late and not call.

170

Men get the chance to sharpen our political skills, and women get a chance to strengthen their creative juices. It's a flip flop of epic proportions that the world benefits from! Not only is it not wrong, it's damn near altruistic.

7. Sleep in the wet spot. We've already established that each gender has an equal stake in making sex a pleasurable experience. From courting to coitus, sex is the world's truest symbiotic activity; an event where much of the outcome is based on creating an environment where teamwork trumps talent and unity usurps uniqueness.

But, the moment the last orgasmic reverberation ends, all notions of gender equality, togetherness, teamwork, and sexual ubuntu end as well. Men are expected to be the sacrificial, *"lay in the mysteriously colored wet spots made as a result of your collective effort to cum"* lambs, ignoring the fact that humans aren't built to lay in random coital dampness.

Yet, despite this blatant and flagrant inequality, *and despite the fact that we're not the ones secreting random water-based lubricants all over the sheets and shit,* we accept this arrangement, as long as you don't ask us to get up and make you any Kool-Aid.

8. Don't complain about our days. We hate our commutes, our bosses, our idiot coworkers, our *"too damn talkative for a fucking Monday morning"* cubicle nemesis, our secretary's terrible brick-based brownies (and the fact that she'll "accidentally" misplace one of our messages if we refuse to eat one of them), the lunchtime lines at Au Bon Pain, the too flirty cashiers, the fact that the one cashier who's actually cute is the one that never

171

flirts with us, and the fact that no one in the office remembered it's our birthday *just as much as you do.*

But, in what may be our most altruistic act, we usually leave it all at the office, allowing you to bask alone in your professional martyrdom glory. Trust me, on the chivalry scale, there's no difference between *walking on the outside of the sidewalk while with a woman* and saying *"My day was fine. Yours?"* when you ask us about our day at work.

9. Investigate the bumps in the night. We really don't want to go see what the noise is. We'd prefer to go to just sleep and hope it ain't there when we wake up. Remember, we were next to you on the couch when you watched that *"Unsolved Mysterious"* episode that scared the living daylights out of you. Newsflash: It scared the hell out of us too![59]

But that won't work for you. So, we risk life, limb, and possible decapitation to make sure that your selfish ass gets to live another day.

---

[59] Still, Robert Stack's voice is nowhere near as scary to us as the following:

1. Having an extremely unattractive daughter. While we'd love her just as much as a cute one, this scares us because we all remember how the ugly girl in school was (mis)treated, and we wouldn't wish that on our worst enemy. With that being said, we'd still rather deal with this than the prospect of...
2. Having an early "developed" and hotpants daughter. Basically, we just hope that any daughter we have will be a nerdy tomboy with a cute face who doesn't grow breasts or booty until she's 22.
3. Knocking up a one-night stand. An unexpected pregnancy is bad enough, but an unexpected pregnancy from the Applebee's waitress you met at the cut-rate is enough to send any sane man to an insane asylum. Seriously, thinking about shit like that makes you want to invest in Kevlar rubbers. Or, you know, actually start wearing them. –*T.C.*

10. Allow you to convince us to try *new* foods. If you were to open the fridge in any random bachelor's apartment today, you'd probably see nothing but myriad representatives from each of the three main food groups—breakfast food, reheatable beef products, and fruity shit stored in the fridge just in case a woman decides to come through. That's it.

But, when we're with you, we're eating Ethiopian lasagna and Thai scrambled eggs and anus-angering Indian food.[60] So what if our stomachs are growling like Busta Rhymes in the "*Scenario*" video, we do it in an attempt to appease your need for *atmosphere* and *newness* and *ambiance* and other dumb-ass sounding descriptive nouns.

11. Leave the toilet seat up. After getting up in the middle of the night and stumbling through the darkness to relieve ourselves, we occasionally forget to put the toilet seat down when finished. Women usually complain about this.

But, if you all knew the actual truth—*if the toilet seat is actually down after we've relieved ourselves in the middle of the night, there's a likely chance the seat was never actually up, which also means there's a likely chance we just said "fuck it" and decided to pee on the toilet seat*—you'd realize exactly how kind and considerate we were to leave it up.

---

[60] Seriously, can someone tell me why Indian food hates our anuses so much? Did our anuses sleep with their sister? Do our anuses own them money? Did our anuses promise Indian food that it would always be its "spiritual son"? If anyone has any idea what their beef is, please let me know. –*T. C.*

173

12. Masturbate. We masturbate (frequently) so we're not as compelled to sleep with each of your friends. This may not seem like much, but when you consider that we're saving you the trouble of having to find a new group of women to borrow dresses from and dread going to Saturday brunch with, this might be our most chivalrous act.

The Impossible Dream
6 Very Smart Ways to (Try to) Keep Your Woman Happy

By The Champ

To dream the impossible dream
to fight the unbeatable foe
to bear with unbearable sorrow
to run where the brave dare not go

To right the unrightable wrong
to love pure and chaste from afar
to try when your arms are too weary
to reach the unreachable star

These lyrics are from "The Impossible Dream", a song featured on *The Man of La Mancha*—a musical based on Miguel de Cervantes's novel "Don Quixote."[61] I'm citing them because whenever I try to think of possible ways to ensure that a woman you're in a relationship with will stay happy (or, at least, content), this song pops in my head, and I can't figure out exactly why. I wonder if my brain is trying to tell me something.

1. Be a cheerleader. Between bearing children, dealing with workforce inequality, suffering through a gauntlet of piss-boy pirouettes, and efficiently navigating a Macy's sales rack on Black Friday, women have a ton on their collective plates.

---

[61] Along with a few songs from *The Man of La Mancha*, I also know all of the words from *Jesus Christ Superstar*. This knowledge is a direct product of my private school education, a fact which is either a ringing endorsement or damning indictment of sending your kids to private school. I haven't figured out which one, yet. –*T.C.*

Because of this, the unspoken household cheerleader duties usually fall on the man. It's our job to be the perpetual pom-pom boy, the public relations specialist assuring her that her butt isn't getting too big and that she's going to ace her real-estate exam, and we need to be optimistic because there's nothing more unproductive and contradictory than a pessimistic cheerleader. There's a reason cheers usually say something like, *"Go Team!"* or *"We're Number One!!!"* instead of *"Dammit Team. Do Something"* or *"We Could Be Number Seven With a Little Bit of Luck!!!"*

Remember, *"Don't worry babe. You'll get that promotion"* works much better than *"Yeah, you're right. I wouldn't give your flighty ass a bonus either."*

2. Occasionally say no for no apparent reason, and refuse to explain yourself.[62]

---

[62] **"Show signs that you might actually be a little bit crazy"** is #1 on the list of "Three sure-fire ways to woo a black woman" The rest?

2. Make it known that you're genuinely interested in and attracted to black women. There are many ways to do this, but the easiest is to just find a group of black women somewhere and let them overhear you make a disparaging comment about a "typically attractive" non-black woman while matter-of-factly lauding the looks of a sista who doesn't fit the usual American standard of beauty. (i.e.: "Eh. Megan Fox is overrated. They need to stop playing and cast my girl Jilly from Philly in *"Transformers 3"*) If this doesn't work, just talk shit about Taye Diggs.

3. Belong to something. Whether it's a fraternity, church, civic organization, or the Crips, for whatever reason, black women seem to be genuinely enthralled by men who belong to some type of group. If I had the time, I'd figure out exactly why, but I'm pretty sure it has something to do with Frankie Lymon. –*T.C.*

176

"Honey, when you go to the store, can you pick up some wheat bread?"

"No."

"Ummm. Okay. Do you want some head?"

This throws them through loops, and makes you seem much more unpredictable, assertive, demonstrative and mysterious than you really are. Chicks love safe loops. It reminds them of breakfast cereal and Six Flags.

3. Freely flatter her looks. Regardless of how confident and self-aware she might seem to be, many, if not most, women are completely neurotic when it comes to their looks. You can blame anything from nature to the alcohol for this, but most do put a harsh premium on how physically and sexually attractive they are because they know that society unfairly is prone to do the same thing.

With this in mind, it's not the worst idea to remind her that you still find her physically and sexually attractive on a regular basis. How you actually construct the compliment depends on their personality. As far as I know, there are five different ways to complete this valuable mission.

A) The sparkling adjective: *"You're beautiful, babe."* Best utilized on a dinner date or right after sex.

B) The matter-of-fact attentiveness: *"Did I ever tell you that you have the sexiest legs?"* Best utilized while watching her walk in the living room with a bag of popcorn.

177

C) The descriptive hyperbole: *"Damn, girl. That dress make yo booty look like a big ass bucket of chicken gravy."* Best utilized if she has two or more gold teeth.

D) The backhanded surprise: *"Damn. Dinner sucked. It would have sucked even more if you weren't so damn good looking."* Best utilized if she has low self-esteem.

E) The aggressively urgent bluntness: *"I need to fuck you, RIGHT NOW!"* Best utilized if you're actually good in bed.

Also, when complimenting her looks, try to give her props for something that isn't readily apparent. For instance, if your woman is busty, a compliment about her eyes or legs will go much further than a remark about her boobs. And, while you've probably been told that you shouldn't ever make a remark to a woman that in any way alludes to her being chunky or gaining weight, it's not the worst idea to give your skinny *"I can't grow a butt to save my life"* girlfriend a compliment about her new curves.[63]

4. Brag about her. They'll probably never admit it, but pretty much every woman secretly desires to be a trophy showpiece, a dark-brown skinned blue ribbon their man makes a personal edict to boast, gloat, and brag about like he won the Powerball.

---

[63] If there are any Very Smart Caucasian—or any other non-black—males reading this, I'd be careful with the whole "complimenting her curves" thing. I might be wrong, but it seems like most white women probably won't take "Damn, girl. You went up a whole pants size in a month? Good for you!!!" as a compliment. –*T.C.*

This isn't suggesting that a showpiece is *all* they want to be, but most women love it when the man they're with does everything he can to promote her uniqueness, beauty, and special talents. Whether it's a simple "*My baby just passed the Bar Exam!!*" Facebook status message or letting her know you think she's the baddest thing in the room at all times, a little bit of flattery goes a very, very, very long way.

5. Listen and shit. Not to every word, of course. *Duh.* I said make her happy, not kill yourself. But, do try to make an effort to pay attention to and heed 35-55% of what she says and she'll be gayer than Christmas morning.[64]

6. Protect the paint. Every great basketball team has had an enforcer; a Charles Oakley or Ron Artest who had everyone's back with the implied notion that they wouldn't hesitate to fuck you up if you were too rough with his teammates. Few things make a woman happier than knowing that her paint is protected, and nothing

---

[64] But, while you're paying attention, make sure to be aware of these popular lies women love to tell.

"You always hit my spot just right." Yeah, okay. You're right. Except really, sex is like *Any Given Sunday*. Sometimes, you have a bad day. But, she's really nice if she tells you this knowing full well she had to finish the job herself AND convince you that you're the man. That's a good lie.

"I've never done that before." Saying you've never done that before usually means you've done it before but you just like to pretend that you didn't do it before because if folks knew how many times you really did it, they might not want you to do it to them. –*P.J.*

induces unprompted morning blow jobs better than a concrete *"I got yo back"* assurance. If more men had their women's backs, there would be more happy relationships. And, like we've repeated numerous times, more happy relationships = less crime.

Basically, if more men had their woman's back during the day, you probably wouldn't have to watch your back when going to the ATM at night.

Not So High Fidelity
Everything You've Ever Wanted to Know About Why (Some) Men Cheat

Part 1: Every Single Possible Reason Why a Man Would Cheat

By The Champ

You know, I've always hated the "Why do men cheat?" question, because the query itself has a way of implying three separate falsehoods.

A) All men cheat.

B) Cheating is a man-specific trait.

C) Men are monoliths who all cheat for the exact same reason.

With that being said, although I've never personally cheated on a mate, I'm especially equipped to answer this because I've been friends and acquaintances with so many habitual cheaters that I consider myself to be a cheating maven. I've been every alibi (*"Yeah Kim, he was with me last Wednesday night. He let me borrow his blender, and since he was here, we watched the Spurs game, did some blow, and fell asleep on my couch"*), heard every story, and had every possible alcohol-induced guilty rationale volunteered to me (*"I know I be doing my girl dirty, dog, but I'm anemic so I can't help it."*)

Basically, I've heard every single logical reason why a man might have cheated. Every. Single. One.

181

While some are mind-numbingly simple and others are much more nuanced and layered than *He's just a selfish bastard* and *He aint shit,* each provides a snapshot into how a man can be convinced to casually or concisely thumb his nose to the idea of monogamy.

1. He thinks being monogamous is unreasonable.[65] Some guys just don't believe being faithful is even possible, so they don't even try. Also, some guys don't believe their vote matters, so they don't even bother to register. Point? Some guys just suck.

2. He just decided to because he was bored. Sometimes, it's really as simple as a guy saying to himself, *"You know, I've never cheated on my girl before. I think I will this weekend after the Steelers game. Maybe I'll stop at Steak 'n Shake afterwards."*

3. He needs the extra attention. There are some men who can't function without women perpetually fawning over him. Once they get past the initial new relationship high, they need more fawning. And, as we all know, fawning sometimes leads to forking.

---

[65] Even if you disregard the "cheating is wrong" thought, the idea of cheating has never even really been a relevant issue for me, for three completely separate and somewhat selfish reasons.

1. It seems too time-consuming.

2. I live in Pittsburgh. While six degrees of separation may connect you to everyone everywhere else, The 'Burgh's unique dynamics make it so that it's somewhere between seven tenths and one and a quarter of a degree of separation here, making cheating a logistical nightmare.

3. Apparently I'm prone to make funny f-faces. I'm already self-conscious enough as it is. I don't need a bunch of off-brand chicks knowing exactly what The Champ looks and sounds like when he's making baby champions.—*T.C.*

4. He's just not physically attracted to his woman anymore. While I've heard and read many attribute a man's infidelity to all sorts of hidden and latent factors, sometimes it's really as simple as *She gained too much weight in the past year, She got older,* or *That chimp attack really didn't do any favors to her face.*

5. He feels entitled to. Coined the *Tony Soprano*—because it seems to be a pretty popular theme among movie mobsters, athletes, and other high-status men—this state of mind is basically a guy saying *"I cheat because I can because I am who I am."* On second thought, maybe I should have coined this the *Popeye.*

6. He can't say no to a woman. Maybe it's latent mommy issues. Maybe it's their form of chivalry. Or, maybe they're just emasculated bitches. Whatever the reasons behind it, there are guys who just can't form their lips to say no to any request from any woman, and they usually end up fucking the first overly forward woman they encounter. These are also usually the guys who have closets full of never worn clothes they bought just because the cute chick at the Sean Jean store convinced him to open a credit line.

7. He wants her to break up with him. This happens when a guy wants to end the relationship, but doesn't have the balls to do it himself. This harkens back to the idea that many of us are just unable to say no to a woman. Even the coldest cat will shiver at the thought of telling a woman he cares about that it's over. And, since cheating is much more fun than stealing her credit card or poisoning her cat, it's a pretty easy choice.

8. He just happened to be horny at a time when she (the other chick) was around and his girlfriend wasn't.

Reason number 324 why long-distance relationships don't work[66]

9. He got caught up in the heat of the moment. Sometimes it's not about anything other than the fact that he happened to be rocking some *"long and late hours at the office intensely working on a project with a somewhat attractive female co-worker* **Goggles"** and got caught up. Basically, you're talking about a mix of **Work Goggles** and **Tired Goggles** (and, if she's in her early 20's, possibly even **College Goggles**)

10. She's boring as hell in bed.

Also known as *"The only reasonable explanation for perpetual relationship troubles of Halle Berry and Jennifer Aniston"*

11. He needs to cheat to keep the relationship happy. This is tricky because a guy does this with his woman's long-term benefit in mind. He's in love and wants to be with her but realizes that he'll get frustrated with her if he

---

[66] Long-distance relationships are only good if you don't really want to be in a relationship, but like to tell people that you have a significant other. It's like being in a committed relationship without the commitment, and it's the relationship version of the woman who tells every undesirable guy she meets at the club that she has a "boyfriend." Anyone who tells you otherwise is either cheating or a woman who refuses to accept the fact that the man she's entrusted her 700 miles away heart to is getting his jalopy on with a pretty young bird every Tuesday after happy hour with his boys. Women have out of town boyfriends. Dudes have out of town "wifeys." Big difference. –P.J.

doesn't use another woman as an outlet. It's like the diabetic who just needs to drink one cookies and cream milkshake every month to keep his levels right. And, really, as long as he's protecting himself while drinking the shake, where's the foul?

12. He thinks he can't please her sexually. As I've mentioned before, generally speaking, we (men) are extremely neurotic about our sexual performance. Basically, take a typical woman's neurosis about her nude body and/or sexual prowess, and multiply that by 5. If we feel like we're not able to fulfill your needs, we consider it to be a personal indictment on our manhood (or lack thereof). This neurosis can lead to us going outside of the relationship for the sexual ego boost. This mindset is related to (some) men's infatuation with virginal women, and, oddly enough, Dallas Cowboy fandom.

13. He doesn't respect her. Easily the slimiest of the reasons for cheating, a man with this mindset treats his woman like shit because he doesn't think she deserves any better (*which doesn't say much for his feelings about himself, actually*). He probably also spits in her coffee when she's not looking.

14. She didn't trust him. When basketball teams instigate full-court man-to-man presses, they don't do it to quickly induce turnovers. No, they increase the pressure to speed up the other team's thought process, a phenomenon that can be mentally and physically fatiguing, resulting in mental and physical errors later in the game. And, like a pressing basketball team, the pressure of a woman always thinking that her boyfriend is going to cheat has the ability to *break* some men. Pressure busts pipes, and forces pipes to break backs.

15. He was pursued and seduced. If drawing a blank on how this would look and sound, just think of something a movie character played by Robin Givens would do. Most guys can put up the "No" fence, but it takes a special individual to stop a relentless she-devil who's determined to hop over that gate. It's like wearing a mask in a room full of people with Swine Flu. It'll help, but the Pussy Flu will eventually get you.

16. She's the mother of his children...and he just doesn't want to do freaky sexual things to someone who is breast feeding his daughter. Plus, you can't exactly say "*Whose pussy is this?*" anymore if your infant son did more damage to her vagina than you ever could.

17. She let him do it before. So, this really shouldn't be a surprise. (More on this in **Part 2**)

18. It's his form of masturbation. Although most women think this is bullshit, for some guys, there's no difference between sex with another chick and jerking off to Bootytalk 182.[67]

19. She stopped having sex with him. Duh! (More on this in **Chapter 27.**)

20. He thinks his penis is his only positive attribute. Basically, this is the guy who ties his entire self-worth on being able to get women off, and he doesn't feel worthy

---

[67] Actually, this *is* bullshit, but I needed to include that line because the BootyTalk people are sponsoring our book tour. —*T.C.*

of living life if he's not able to do that with multiple women. It's all he thinks he's good at. And, as porn star Brian Pumper's[68] multiple "attempts" at "rapping" prove, if he feels this way, he's probably right.

21. He always needs to win. Some ultra-competitive alpha male types can't stand losing, ever. To him, he cheats because he wants to win every attractive girl he sees for himself, *just so that the other guys interested in her will lose.* Not only do they not mind collateral damage, they thrive on it. It's probably how he got his current girlfriend as well, but she was too awed by his alpha-ness to notice or even care about the casualties left by his pursuit of her.

22. He's been in a relationship for an extended period of time, and he needed to see if he's still attractive to other women. Out of all the reasons listed, this is the one I sympathize with the most. Even during moments of relationship bliss, there have been times when I've wished that I was single for a day just to see if I was still able to pick up women. It's the proverbial guy on a business trip who takes off his wedding ring before heading to the hotel bar. But, while I do understand the mindset behind this, a man could probably pull this off without actually sleeping with other women.

---

[68] There are few people in, well, *life* who induce the types of conflicting emotions from anyone that the subject of Brian Pumper manages to emit from black porn connoisseurs. Some laud him for his marketing acumen and his ability to consistently inject his porn series with new and attractive talent. Others — *including other* porn *stars* — think he's a weirdo and closet homosexual whose blatant (and, occasionally, hilarious) narcissism make any scene he's featured in completely unwatchable. Basically, he's the black porn version of Diddy. –*T.C.*

23. He found someone he likes more than her, and he just hasn't broken up with her yet. Shit happens.

24. He was peer pressured into it. It's rare, but there are guys who cheat just because everyone else in their peer group is doing it. You'd be amazed at how much a guy's peer group influences their romance relationships. There's a reason why most guys tend to get married (or divorced) in groups. Birds of a feather flock and fuck chickenheads together.

25. You cheated on him. Duh, again.

26. He's a sex addict.[69] While I'm sure thousands of men have tried to use this as a copout, sex addictions do actually exist. They even have support groups and VH1 reality shows and shit for them. Who knew that Tiger Woods—and the fact that he entered some sort of $10,000 a day sex addiction retreat a couple of months after the golf club incident—would save the relationships of men across the country? Now, a cheating man can hit his woman with a *"I have an addiction. I'm sick. Would you break up with me if I had cancer, too?"* guilt trip.

27. He's a thrill seeker. To him, sex isn't fulfilling unless he knows he's doing something or someone he shouldn't be doing. If you're a woman who recently broke up with a sexual thrill seeker, make sure you get tested, and you should probably also take your pets to the veterinarian.

---

[69] According to a recent study led by Justin Garcia, a SUNY Doctoral Diversity Fellow at Binghamton University, there may be a genetic disposition to infidelity. Not sure if I completely buy this, but man, what if Eric Benet had used this science during his divorce proceedings to state that he didn't cheat on Halle on purpose...*he got it from his daddy?* Shit, maybe he'd actually still have a career. –*P..J.*

28. He was given an offer or opportunity he couldn't refuse. How many other times will he have the opportunity to have a threesome with Stacey Dash and Nia Long? Shit, I think most straight women (and gay men) wouldn't even pass that up.

29. He couldn't choose between his girlfriend/wife and the other chick, so he just decided to have both. To a man in this position, doing this is no different than going to Cold Stone Creamery and saying, *"Damn, I can't choose between Sweet Cream and Moosetracks. Maybe I'll just get both."* If you're a woman and this happens to you, just hope that he considers *you* to be Sweet Cream.

I actually think either Usher or R. Kelly has an entire album devoted to this scenario, an album named either *"Deceitful Decisions"* or *"The Coochie Conundrum."* I can't remember which.

30. He's intentionally self-destructive. He knowingly does shit to sabotage good around him and he can't help it. If it's not cheating, it'll be something else. With this in mind, look at the bright side: Cheating is better than arson.

31. He wanted to hurt her to pay her back for something she did to him. Every woman reading should remember this the next time you publicly scold your man about him not putting down the toilet seat.

32. He has more options now than he did when they first met each other. You know, being aware of the state of mind behind this train of thought helps me understand why, 80 years ago, men seemed to be much more eager to marry at a young age than we are now.

If you grew up in the 1930s, the only women you'd see in the first 18 years of your life lived within a 5 mile radius. It was easier to pick a mate because, well, you just didn't have that many to choose from. It's like going to a shoe store that only carries one shoe, but in three different colors. Sure, the shoe you'd pick would probably fit you just fine, but not too many people would stay completely confident in that choice if they walked into a Nike outlet the next day and saw 1,000 different available and attractive choices. The guy who suddenly has much more access to different types of women is the customer at the Nike outlet; a man so overloaded with new information that instead of just trying on the new shoes, he fucks them. No wonder they always ask you to keep on your socks.

33. He was with her before he even met his current girlfriend. I have a friend who has had the exact same side chick in each of his last three relationships. He finds, dates, and gets in relationships with other women while keeping the exact same chick on the sidelines.

Honestly, this is one I don't understand. I'm going to have to get him on the VerySmartBrothas.com podcast one day to explain himself.

34. He needed to get it out of his system before fully committing. Although this seems like another *sounds like bullshit* excuse, it actually does occasionally ring true. Some men have monogamy on their bucket lists, so they cheat one last time to be able to be fully confident in the fact that they'll actually be faithful for the rest of their lives.

190

Look, I said I was going to give reasons. *"Giving reasons"* doesn't mean *"only give reasons that make sane and rational sense."*

35. He enjoys getting over on people. Jimmy Conway— Robert Deniro's character in *Goodfellas*—was introduced to the audience as a person who loved stealing so much that he'd rather steal something than get it for free. (I actually know a few people like that. But, instead of calling them *Goodfellas,* I know them as *People from Harlem.*)

There are men (and women) who treat sex this exact same way. They cheat because of the rush they get when knowing they know something their mate doesn't know. If a woman is involved with a guy like this, cheating is the last of her concerns since he probably has been embezzling money from her savings account since their second date.

Part 2: Why So Many of Us (Rightly) Think We'll Get Away With It

By Panama Jackson

To fully grasp the state of mind and circumstance that allows a man to believe that cheating is a-okay, allow me to take you to a magical and mystical place far, far, far, far away. Yup, we're going to the hood.

Setting: A booth at a random check cashing/fried chicken spot in North Philadelphia. Ashinkashay Jenkins has just found out that her boyfriend, Dontelodolphus Wilkins, has been cheating on her. The proof was in the form of a few text messages and graphic pictures Ashinkashay found on

191

Dontelodolphus's Cricket phone. No collateral damage was involved (read: Dontelodolphus didn't cheat on Ashinkashay with any of her friends) but cheating definitely occurred.

Ashinkashay: *"I can't believe you cheated on me! How could you? After all we've been through. I gave you money. I made you an extra key. I helped you study for your Pre-Paid Legal salesman exam. I swallowed. I even pretended to like your godson's stupid-ass demo tape. This is how you repay me, motherfucker?"*

Dontelodolphus: *"Baby, I'm sorry. I didn't mean to hurt you. I mean, one moment I was in Wine and Spirits, getting some whiskey and pretzels, and the next moment, I have the saleslady in a naked pretzel in the back room. I blacked out. It'll never happen again. I promise baby. Put down the barbeque sauce and that knife so we can talk."*

A: *"Get out!!!!!!!!!! Get yo' shit...get yo' shit, and GET OUT!!!!!!!!!!!!!!!"*

D: *"Um, you realize we're not home now, right?"*

A: *"I don't care where the hell we are!!!! We could be on the damn moon for all I care. Get yo' shit and get out, motherfucker!!!!"*

D: *"Wait, why do you keep calling me 'motherfucker'?"*

A: *"Get out!!!!"*

Now Ashinkashay had this right. He cheated, and she's supposed to let his ass go. You can't teach an old dog new tricks, especially if the old dog has been sleeping with old tricks. But wait, there's more.

The next day: Ashinkashay talks to her friend, Creshenka, and professes that she loves Dontelodolphus more than life.

Ashinkashay: *"How could he do this to me?"*

Creshenka: *"Fuck that nigga and come get twisted with me tonight."*

A: *"I mean, I baked this fool a whole chicken every Sunday. A whole chicken!!! Do you know how many crackheads I had to rob to get him a whole chicken every week? You can't buy that type of love."*

C: *"I know. That's why you need to hit the club with me tonight. Fuck these analog-ass niggas. Maybe you can come back to my place after the club, and maybe we can…"*

A: *"But, he did say he'd change. And, I love him. I even got a tattoo on my back last week with a picture of him and the words, "And, I love him," printed underneath. And, he did say he'd change."*

C: *"Whatever. Take his sorry ass back. Just don't be calling me crying and shit the next time he fucks a chick at the dollar store. But, in the meantime, you can still come through tonight if you want to play spades or cuddle or something."*

Ashinkashay calls Dontelodolphus a week later.

A: *"I'm so hurt that you would do this to me? Why? Don't the chickens even matter?"*

D: *"I don't know, baby. I wasn't thinking. I'm sorry baby, I miss you. I promise it will never happen again."*

A: *"You promise?"*

D: *"Yes. Now, can we please get past this?"*

A: *"Okay, baby. But, if you do this again...it's over!!!"*

D: *"Okay, baby. Now let's go get some baked chicken and have some baked chicken sex."*

Do you see what just happened there? He got away with it! Not only did she not make him pay for the cheating, she practically invited his baked chicken eating ass back, and all it took was a half-hearted promise that he wouldn't do it again.

Ladies, ladies, ladies, can we rap for a second? Sweet. Now, when your child acts up, you pop his ass. When your friend acts up or does something to violate your trust, you cut her back. Why? Well, you don't need to have someone in your life that you can't trust, so you act accordingly!

However, some of you find it in your heart to look past a cheating mate, just because he said he would change and because you hate not having someone to warm up the bed for you before you jump in it. Ladies, ladies, ladies, he tried you and won. And, it all stems from the fact that somewhere along the way, this cat probably cheated on some woman and she let him back into her life. She eventually broke up with him, he found you, cheated again, and you go and do the same thing she did. Now, this cat has no reason not to cheat. He knows if he finds

194

some fine ass woman and sleeps with her, you'll let him stay if he happens to get caught. Shit, why not??? You can have your cake and eat it too. Tell her you're going to change, that you weren't yourself, apologize, yada yada yada. Badaboom badabing! In like Flynn. He hasn't been made to pay for his cheating, therefore, in his mind, it's almost worth it to try. You'd be wise to bet that Dontelodolphus will just do his best to not get caught again.

Although this took place in the hood, this situation plays itself out across the country on a daily basis. Some dude cheats on his girl, gets caught, spits a little game and somehow manages to find himself back into her life for dinner. The first time a man cheats on a woman...and gets away with it, you better believe dude is shook. He might act cool, but he's thinking to himself "WHAT THE SHIT JUST HAPPENED HERE???" It's like when your parents caught you stealing cookies as a youngster and you knew you should have been punished but they don't punish you. There is a grace period where you're on your P's and Q's because you really don't understand what the hell just happened.

But, you know what? The scared-ness wears off. And, you try it again, thinking "Well, I got away with it once...why not twice?" Of course you try to hide your tracks a little bit better, but you almost want to get caught to see what will happen this time. And, when the pain doesn't come? FIESTA, BITCHES!

Now, I know there's a segment of women out there who won't take that shit and I applaud that because, well, there seems to be a whole lot more who will scour the

Earth to find an excuse for the dude they're with.[70] If the dude keeps cheating, eventually the woman will get tired of it and leave. But, by that point, she's usually so bitter that she won't ever trust a man again, even when she gets married; all because somewhere along the line, that dude got away with cheating in the first place. Dontelodolphus? Like the movie Groundhog Day, he'll be doing the exact same thing soon enough. This could happen to you! Let him cheat and you could potentially be the cause of another woman's disappointment later on in life. They say cheaters never prosper. But, they obviously never met Dontelodolphus.

---

[70] Cheating isn't the only "exception" —deal-breakers women will look past if they're interested in you—I've seen them make.

1. **Kids.** I can't tell you how many women will tell you they don't want to date a man with a kid...until you tell them you have a kid. Then, all of a sudden it's "Well, not two kids...wait, how many did you say you have because my cut off is whatever you said?"

2. **Opposing Religious Views.** Most (black) women will tell you they want a man to go to church with them every Sunday. Then, you drop the, "Yeah, well I don't go to church and have no intention of doing so." Without missing a beat, she'll reply "Well you do believe in God right? Because as long as that's the case, I'll look past the fact that church really matters to me and you'd never go with me. I have cable, too."

3. **Unemployment.** The vast majority of women will tell you they want a man with a job...until they meet that jobless starving artist who happens to look just like Derek Jeter. Then, all of a sudden "ambition" is more important than the actual financial manifestation of dollarage. –P.J.

Cheat, Shiiet
A Very Smart Rant from The Champ

Although I staunchly believe there's **absolutely nothing** you can do to keep someone from cheating, there are a few ways that you can push them closer to the edge. You can't actually drive someone to cheat, but you can definitely buy the car, carry them to the driver's seat, and put the keys in the ignition.

1. Romance, schmoemance. You didn't realize it, but you started having sex with her at 8:45 in the morning while she was on the bus headed to work. No, you didn't actually physically have a morning quickie in the passenger aisle of the EBA transit bus, but that little *"Mornin, cutie-pie. Sexy ass...damn. Nevermind."* text you sent her made her smile and produced the first tiny drop of anticipation moisture *down there* that will continue to accumulate throughout the day.

The 1:17 pm text saying *"I have a surprise for you later on"*? **More drops.**

Being early for the date, and softly kissing her when you see her, pulling her close enough so that she can tell you're wearing her favorite cologne, but not so close that she can feel your lil' general standing at attention? **Leaky faucet.**

Opening your car door for her, while gently guiding her in; your hand slightly beneath the small of her back? **Brazilian rainforest.**

At this point, she's not even thinking about anything else other than, *"Please, please, please God don't let him do anything dumb tonight to mess this up,"* and your work is done. Going from a consistent serving of **that...**

...to this...

You: *"Come over and let me hit. And, on the way, stop and get me some fries...and condoms. Peace, homie."*

Her: *"It's 9:47, and I haven't heard from you all day."*

You: *"Damn...Yeah, you're right. You better hurry then. Wendy's drive-thru is gonna be closed soon."*

...will soon get you a one-way ticket on the *"I wonder why my girlfriend just rubbed the mailman's ass and smiled"* express.

2. Stop having sex, stupid. There's no lonelier place in the world than a bed where your mate has decided, for whatever reason, to stop having sex with you. And, there is no better and no more efficient way to put the cheating key in the ignition. Honestly, it's actually easier sleeping next to a mate you've never slept with than one who all of a sudden decided to rock their rusty-ass chastity belt to bed. Unless you have some type of serious physical or emotional impairment, **the reasoning behind intentionally inducing a prolonged sex spell never matters.** It's always stupid, you're always stupid for doing this, and it's just plain fucking stupid.

I'm on long-term punany punishment 'cause you're mad at me? *Fuck you! Fuck me.* You've all of a sudden started believing that I'm only with you for the sex? *Fuck you! Fuck me.* You've decided out of the blue to become born again and celibate? *Fuck you! Fuck me.*

Of course, I understand that grown-ass people occasionally have libido-deading responsibilities that realistically don't allow for spider monkey mummy matrix sex every day of the week. Shit, I never thought I'd say this, but sometimes during my meetings at work, instead of daydreaming about some combination of a naked Stacey Dash, a car seat, and a universal remote, I'm sitting there literally fantasizing about the nasty things I plan to run home and do to my...pillow. Sleep sometimes trumps sex, and that's okay. Still, if the pillow-bating doesn't stop, your mate is either going to not cheat...but want to cheat, *not cheat...but only because they haven't had the opportunity to,* or cheat.

3. Be like Ike. Isaac "Ike" Austin was a somewhat decent power forward/center for the Miami Heat and the LA Clippers in the mid-90's. Originally passed over and cut by many teams when first leaving college, he went to Europe for a year to refine his skills, and eventually returned to the NBA a much better player. He made such improvement that he actually won the NBA's most improved player award in 1997. This improvement eventually led to him being offered a very lucrative multi-year contract with the Orlando Magic.

So, did Ike continue to improve after he finally got his big payday? **Nah. He got fat, his game got worse, and he was out of the league within three years.**

If you want to ensure that your mate will *thirst for cheating on you,* **be like Ike.** Do everything you can to break the implied relationship contract you agreed to when you first got together. Gain 50 pounds. Stop bathing. Start wearing your late uncle's clothes. End all oral. Get giant tear drop tats on your Adam's apple. Do everything you can to make them believe that they were a fool for committing to you. **Be like Ike.**

Jazmine Sullivan Might End Your Life
A Very Smart Rant from Panama Jackson

"I bust the windows out ya car
And no it didn't mend my broken heart
I'll probably always have these ugly scars
But right now I don't care about that part

I bust the windows out ya car
After I saw you laying next to her
I didn't wanna but I took my turn
I'm glad I did it 'cause you had to learn..."

—Lyrics from "Bust Your Windows", a not so Very Smart song by Jazmine Sullivan.

Ladies and gentlemen, I'm afraid. I'm afraid that vehicle property damage is going to increase by at least 8% in the next few months. But, there is some good news about this. I just saved 15% by switching my car insurance to Geico. And, the funny part is that it's completely true. I called Geico and they cut my car insurance down by over 100 bucks.

So Jazmine, if you and your insane fem-mob decide to bust the windows in my car, I'm covered. However, let's discuss this a little bit, okay?

Okay, dude's a douche-bag. That's true. Break up with him. Call the game. Forfeit the love. Unfortunately, she can't do that. She must get revenge. She throws on some Blu Cantrell, "Hit 'Em Up Style," and decides that writing her name in the hood of his car with a crowbar is a good idea. And, oh yeah...she busts the window of his car.

201

Look, I jokingly reference the insanity of women on a daily basis. It's a well documented fact that a lot of women are, indeed, off their proverbial rockers. But you know who's really crazy? Like really, really? A black man who's had his shit unnecessarily fucked the hell up. Oh yeah, that ninja is insane. In life, what every relationship-minded straight black woman should want—apart from a man with a good job, good credit, and a penis at least proportional to his height and weight—is a man who is afraid of jail. Ladies, take this one to the bank: If you meet a man who is honestly not afraid of doing a bid in jail...**leave him.** Immediately. As in, end the date, and call the cops because he probably already has at least seven outstanding warrants.

Now, let's say you do manage to date a man who is afraid of jail when you meet him. Like most sane black men over age 14, dude realizes he has something to lose in life. But, we all have our breaking points. That's word. Life.

"I must admit it helped a little bit
To think of how you'd feel when you saw it
I didn't know that I had that much strength
But I'm glad you see what happens when
You see you can't just play with peoples feelings
Tell them you love them but don't mean it
You probably say that it was juvenile
But I think that I deserve to smile"

In the second verse of this song, Sullivan gets her jollies by imagining what dude's going to say when he sees his car. In her mind, he'll be pissed and upset, and he'll ultimately realize the error of his ways. And, you know what, two out of three really ain't bad.

However, that last one is sooooo not happening. It's especially not happening while he's on the way to find you while his homeboy tries to convince him to calm down and not do anything crazy. See, there really is nothing good to come of ruining his car. Nobody wins there.

Plus, as I pointed out in **Part 2** of **Not So High Fidelity,** you probably still want him anyway. You just want other people to think that you don't so you can look strong. It's why songs like this and Beyonce's "Single Ladies" are such crocks of shit. For many (if not most) women, hope springs eternal. Despite all the wrong that's been done you, there is still that glint of hope that the man will "come to his senses" and realize what he has/had and make the best decision he can make...*to be with the woman who just busted the windows of his car.* This is actually one of the many reasons why I love women. No matter how much some of us put them through, many of them still want the man they put so much time into so they don't have to start over, *"Ugly Girl Problems"* personified.[71]

---

[71] What are "ugly girl problems?" Well, it describes women who deal with repeated nonsense from men and refuse to exercise their option to not deal with such fuckery for no good reason other than attempts to not be lonely. Basically, it's what happens when women act like the man they're with is the only man on Earth they can possibly be with, even if he's a shitty man. Here's a word of advice to all the women out there who get attention from men and yet constantly end up dealing with the wrong dude for a long time: Realize that you have options. I like women brown, yellow, Puerto Rican, and Haitian. And, most men do too. I don't want to hear about no shortage. That only affects mudducks and goats without thunder. Why sit at a bar waxing philosophical with your girls about why the dude won't call you back when you have some other guy literally blowing up your phone? It breaks my heart. –*P.J.*

But, you can't have him. He's on the way to make you dead for busting the windows of his car. You wanted him to feel some emotion, now you got some. And, you better hope that dude comes to his senses and wants to see Obama get re-elected while he's on the way to find you.

The Do's and Don'ts of Breaking Up...
...and What to Do If They Don't Get the Hint

By The Champ and Panama Jackson

We're all messed up. And, again, it's all Hollywood's fault. You see, being raised on a steady diet of shit like *The War of the Roses, Waiting to Exhale,* and *Fatal Attraction* led us to believe that all romantic break-ups were brutal bloodfeuds; complete with vicious insults, violent threats, hateful feelings, torn rabbits, microwaved weave, and blonde women somehow lurking in the background. This faulty expectation left us ill-equipped and unprepared for real life, where the vast majority of adult break-ups occur while both parties still have generally positive feelings towards each other, a fact that occasionally turns this simple process into a prolonged lesson in passive-aggressive bitchassedness.

With this in mind, here are a few tips to remember to make the breaking-up process easier for you and everyone else involved.

1. Do it face to face. Unless, of course, they're licensed to carry.

2. Don't be scared to let them hate you. There's nothing worse than allowing someone to still think they have a chance because you're prolonging the process, motivated by the fear that they're going to hate you. Wait, Diddy solo albums are worse, but you get my point. Man or Woman up and break the news.

3. Don't call them every five minutes to curse them out. Along with making you look and feel like an ass, this is

205

just going to make them even surer that the break-up was the right decision. As upset as you might be about the break-up now, trust that you'll be 100 times more upset with yourself two months later if you allow yourself to do this. Plus, you're expending a lot of energy you could be putting to more constructive activities, like masturbation or perfecting your orange Kool-Aid.

4. Don't watch every sappy-ass romantic movie you can think of. Why torture yourself? Plus, chances are, you didn't really have that romance in the first place. You weren't Tre and Brandy (*Boyz in the Hood*) or even Mickey and Mallory (*Natural Born Killers*). You were probably more like Treach and Lisa-Nicole Carson (*Jason's Lyric*).

5. Do make sure that they're the first to know. Let's just say that it's probably not the best idea to discuss your plans in a conference call with her mom and stepdad a week before you tell her. It's also probably not a good idea to put it on YouTube.

6. Don't re-read every letter and/or email you have from them saved in their special folder.

7. At the same time, don't delete them all either. What else are you going to read on those lonely Sundays? You're alone now, so you need to do something to keep your lonely-ass occupied.

8. Don't explain exactly why…unless they ask. If so,

9. Do lie. They say honesty is the best policy. They also told me that Tupac was still alive and recording albums in Guyana. Basically, they are full of shit. Unless this

206

person has a serious impairment that can actually be fixed, there's no reason to let somebody know that you left them because her sister's ass was fatter or you got tired of the way his neck smelled.

10. Do not follow them like they're step-by-step directions from Google Maps on Facebook, MySpace, or Twitter. You'll never see what you want to see and you'll see everything you don't want to see, whether or not there's actually anything to see. Basically, it's exactly like going to a strip club locker room.

11. If they have a blog or Twitter account, don't read it everyday looking for some glimmer of hope that they're going to write about how they miss you. They don't. They're going to write and tweet about Beyonce and Jay-Z—who are, you know, still together.

12. Don't do any public executions. Break-ups should be done as discreetly as possible, with you two as the only audience. Don't agree? Just ask Lebron James and (Cleveland Cavaliers owner) Dan Gilbert.

With that being said, I'd stay away from secluded areas like the woods, the desert, or Detroit just to quell any temptation of murdering you.

13. Do actually break up. Don't get on some bullshit about taking a break if you really want to let the relationship ride. You see, *breaks* are the dumbest shit known to man. If you're ready to move on, do it. Don't keep the other person hanging onto your proverbial nuts for no reason; mostly because that gives them just cause to slash your tires or kick your puppy off a random bridge like Jack Black in *Anchorman*.

14. Don't pretend that you're not broken up either. It's just not a good look. Just how we know a black person when we see one (don't believe that *Imitation of Life* nonsense), people can sniff out a delusional person like a dog in heat.

15. Do move on, but don't sleep with his or her friends. Admittedly, we think all bets are off at some point. If a lengthy amount of time has passed and their friend is still trying to offer up the snappy nappy dugout (word to Ice Cube), then by all means, there's another hit, Barry Bonds.

16. Don't call them, period. Calling the person you've broken up with just leads to mixed messages. And, since we can't start cloning Nick Cannon to marry them all, the world doesn't need any more confused Mariah Careys running around.

17. Don't hold them to plans you made while you were still together. We know that rolling solo to the family BBQ is going to garner questions. In fact, one of the reasons you actually decided to get in a relationship was to keep your great Aunt Lucy from suspecting that you were gay. However, you broke up so you need to deal with the consequences. And, if this means there's a great chance that, at Thanksgiving dinner, you'll overhear Aunt Lucy talking to your mom and asking if you were a carpet-muncher, buy some ear plugs. If that doesn't work, just steal Aunt Lucy's dentures.

18. If you can, do make it an amicable split, but don't patronize the other person. Don't be nice just for the hell of it and make it seem like you're showing pity on the other person despite the fucked up situation you're in.

However, if you can make it an amicable split, you may still be able to hit when you need a little bit of that good lovin'...or your batteries run out...or your internet connection times out...or something.

19. Don't send them a letter outlining everything that was wrong with them. For one, you rule out all future nakedness.[72] For two, it stands to reason that you'll get a letter in return. And, unless you want to read 300 different ways of saying *"you have a small Johnson"* or *"your breath smells like you just ate a Newark bus driver,"* you should probably fall back, or they'll just show up and stab you.

20. No matter how good the relationship, don't call their friends or their mama. Even if you loved her momma's roast beef, if you break up with somebody, you break up with the roast beef too.

21. Do some self-reflection on the lost relationship, and don't assume that literally just looking in the mirror counts. Try to pragmatically and practically find out what went wrong, and fix it. If it can't be fixed, well, the clergy could always use a few more good men and women.

Now, we both realize that ending a romantic relationship is one of the most difficult things to do. Actually, that's a lie. Like we stated before, it's not really that difficult, it's just that most people at the end of their relationship ropes don't want to be the bad guy, especially if the

---

[72] Yes, we know this contradicts the whole *"don't send mixed messages"* thing, but whatever. Stop hatin'. Sometimes, a little "ex-loving" aint a bad thing. Plus, we all know that most women prefer comfortable cock to new nuts, so it's a win-win. –*P.J.*

relationship malaise hasn't been caused by any egregious sin like cheating, abuse, or a professed admiration for rapper Jim Jones from the Dipset.[73] Sometimes, you just want out, but you don't want to be the one to do it. So, as your last act of relationship kindness, we understand wanting to give the person the pleasure of breaking up with you first. And, we also understand that sometimes your mate is an asshole who has it coming, and you need him to break-up with you first so you'll finally be able to get out of that joint lease. Either way, here are a few ways to accomplish your goal.

1. Be Sarah Palin. With even the smallest real or perceived slight, reply matter-of-factly with the cruelest, most ignorant, and most random insult you could possibly imagine...while smiling. Example:

"My bad honey, I forgot to buy grape Kool-aid."

"Babe, how can a grown man's dick be so little? Seriously, baby cakes, how does that happen? Did your grandfather lose a bet with God or something? When you pee, does it hit your balls on the way down?"

Or

---

[73] My virulent animus for rapper Jim Jones stems from a MTV program I saw him on a few years ago. It was one of those "year in review" type shows; 120 minutes or so of roundtable discussion of many of the top stories in hip-hop that year. One of the stories brought up was the reconciliation of Nas and Jay-Z—two prominent hip-hop icons who apparently decided to get over their silly beef with each other. While everyone else sitting at the table lauded Jigga and Nas for basically growing up, Jim Jones sat with a look on his face like an elephant just farted on his lap. I've never seen a person so thoroughly disgusted about a good thing, and that haterade-filled moment—the very antithesis of Very Smartness—made Jim Jones my personal arch nemesis forevermore. –T.C.

"I'll be maybe 10 minutes late picking you up today."

"You know, sweetie, you're too ugly for me to ever consider having kids with you. I thought you were an anomaly, but after seeing your mom, I know it runs in your wretched family, and baby, I don't want to be infected with your sad, sad joke of a gene pool."

2. Practice intentional sack wackness. Don't cheat and upset the relationship karma Gods, but do everything in your power to ensure that this person never wants to have sex with you ever again.

Climax in seven pumps. Ride lazier than Shaq's left eye. Scream **"Jeopardy!"** pull out, and run a lap around the bed whenever you smack her ass. Attempt to give head with a mouth full of chocolate cake. During missionary, abruptly stop, pull out, get dressed and go on your couch and watch TV, all without saying a word. Instead of *"Daddy,"* incorporate names of other family members when it's getting good, preferably *"Cousin Jack"* or *"Auntie."*

3. Respond to every question or statement with the exact same phrase. It doesn't matter. He asked how your day was. She wants to know what groceries she should get at the store. Regardless of the topic, continue to respond with the exact same sentence each time. *"Whatever floats your boat, queen bee"* and *"Who cares about it all anyway, ever"* seem to work best.

4. Report any and every intimate thing that you do together on the internet. That intense lunch quickie you had earlier in the week? Put it up on Rude.com. That issue she's having with her sister's kids? Create a topic

211

about it on Twitter. That 2,000 word email he sent you, expressing dismay about the direction his life was headed? Post it as a note on Facebook, under the title, *"How should I respond?"* Bonus points if you include dates, real names, and high resolution pictures.

5. Tell them that you're sexually attracted to their sibling or friends. Ladies, make sure your man knows that you think his brother is a motherfucking stallion, Mandingo looking Negro. Brothas, make sure to let your girl know about every time you've fantasized about her homegirl and the outfit she was rocking in each fantasy.

6. Provide evidence that you used to be kind of gay. While this is usually a fool-proof ploy for a guy to get himself dumped, ladies should be especially careful with saying this, because there are guys out there who will actually look at this as a deal-maker, not a deal-breaker. If this happens, just tell him that you slept with his sister.

7. Become a religious zealot and damn them to hell. No one wants to go to hell over some pussy or penis. Purgatory? Maybe. Baltimore? Probably not. Hell? Definitely not.

Daddy's Girls
Uncut and Unfiltered Relationship Advice We Hope to Eventually Give Our Daughters

By The Champ and Panama Jackson

As we alluded to in the intro to this book, we don't believe that women should carry around concretized dating rulebooks in their heads, complete with complex formulas detailing the minimum number of prepositional phrases a man must incorporate per paragraph if he wants a chance to date you a second time, and this would also include our daughters.[74] Yet, as Very Smart Brothas with numerous positive and negative dating experiences and a wealthy war chest of male insight, we'd be remiss if we didn't tell them about a few salient points we'd want them to always remember.

What separates *"advice we'd give our actual daughters"* from *"advice we'd give any random woman"*? Well, our relationship advice tends to come from a more global, crime-fighting perspective. Even if we're advising

---

[74] While this is a chapter devoted to things we will eventually teach our grown daughters, here are a few things that having a baby girl taught me.

1. Girls projectile pee too. One day, I attempted to change my daughter's diaper, until all of a sudden a rainbow of golden liquid cleared at least 8 feet in my room. Then, she pooped at me (yes, AT me). Let's just say, this little lady was having a ball.

2. I don't mind not breastfeeding. I'd read some books about men feeling left out of the process because they can't breastfeed. Fuck them cats. I'm SO cool on that one. It looks like you're getting your Johnson caught in a door and nobody can pry it open.

3. I don't remember nearly as many nursery rhymes as I thought I did. I've come up with and sang more remixes to old songs than has to be legal. Right now, I'm actually waiting on R. Kelly to call me so we can do the nursery rhyme remix album. *–P.J.*

213

women, we usually offer advice that'll make the dating and relationship game easier for women *and* men to navigate.

Our daughters, on the other hand? Shiiiiiiiiiiieeeet. Fuck the globe. It's all about them. Plus, you can be as blunt with your kid as you want without worrying about minor details like political correctness, tact, lawsuits, or getting shanked.

1. "Trust me. You'll know if a man is truly interested and into you." How?

A) He calls you to talk about absolutely nothing. You know what we're talking about. Those asinine conversations about whose toenails are longer and the fact that Sideshow Bob was really the most complex and dynamic character in the history of network television. Any dude willing to sit and engage you in those conversations is interested.

B) He wants to take you everywhere to meet everyone. If he's truly into you, you'll never get the feeling that he's trying to "hide" you from anyone, even if your new hairdo makes you look like a damn fool.

C) He hasn't seen you naked yet, but he's always willing to do whatever it takes to see you, even if that just means standing on your front porch to talk. I can't stress this enough, but anytime a man never feels like he's going out of his way to do something for you, he's sprung. Seriously, if you asked a guy who's truly into you to get you some Cambodian breast milk for your billy goat, "*Whole or skim?*" would be his next question, followed immediately by "*When can I see you again?*"

214

2. "Pay attention to my friends and I so that you'll learn how to recognize a good dude"[75] For clarity, here are a few things (besides shit like, *"He loves his momma,"* *"He doesn't steal your shit,"* and *"He hasn't slept with your niece"*) that all good dudes have in common.

A) His close friends are also good dudes. Basically, if a guy is repeatedly telling you stories about his best friend, and this best friend sounds more triflin' than eating food with utensils on the bus to work, **run.**

Also, most **good dudes** have at least a few friends that they've known since childhood. Beware of the man whose close friends are all *new.* You see, **good dudes** are **good dudes** because they have character, and guys who have character are usually also great judges of character in others. **Good dudes** realize that high character friends are hard to find, which is why most **good dudes** will do everything they can to keep those other high character friends in their circle.

B) He actually likes women. You'd be amazed at how many women we've seen who were interested in and/or in relationships with men who **hated** their entire gender. **Good dudes** *actually like women* and treat them with respect, regardless of if it's his mom, a chick he's trying to sleep with, or the waitress at IHOP.

---

[75] Please note that it's **"good dude"** and not **"nice guy."** There is a difference. Of course, being nice (at times) is good, but Stringer Bell from "The Wire" was nice to women too. –T.C.

215

C) He has at least one "checker." Regardless of their age, all **good dudes** have at least one person who can **"check"** them if need be. Whether it's a parent, a former coach, an older cousin, a teacher, or whatever, every **good dude** has someone in their life that can put them in place if they ever manage to get out of pocket. "Superwoman," a regular commenter at VerySmartBrothas.com, put it best in a comment she left on one of our blog posts in 2009:

"BEWARE of guys who have no family authority/or mentor figures they respect. If it's not their dad, then their older brother, uncle, priest, boss, teacher, mentor - SOMEONE who can talk sense into him when he's bugging out, or in need of guidance in difficult times. If he is one of those people who 'no one can talk to', as is my asshole ex-bro-in-law, then stay far, far, far, FAR away.... a man who respects nobody will wind up disrespecting YOU."

D) He's loyal to the right shit. Whether it's his boys, his barber,[76] or his ballteam, one mark of a good dude is the fact that he's able to keep stable relationships with certain male institutions, instead of being the cat who's always quick to immerse himself in fly-by-night fads. We're not saying that he couldn't or shouldn't evolve,

---

[76] Unless you rock a baldy, every grown ass black man needs to have a barber to keep him looking professional and presentable. Hell, the only person higher up on the ladder than a Black man's barber should be his mother. In fact, a ninja-barber relationship is so important (and fragile) that I just stopped going to my barber years ago because I didn't have the heart to tell him that I was going to shave my own head from here on out. He might actually think I'm dead.

If you're reading this, Rufus Thompkins from Tommy's Cutz on the corner of 5th and MLK, breathe easy now. I'm alive. –P.J.

216

but jumping from bandwagon to bandwagon isn't synonymous with personal evolution.

Also, getting back to the ballteam statement, pay special attention to how he views sports. If he's been a die-hard fan of a team since childhood, he's probably loyal to a fault and also a bit stubborn. If you're watching him play basketball at the park and he's the ball-hog who's pissing off all of his teammates by attempting all of the latest And-1 Mixtape/Streetball tricks during the games, he's probably an immature asshole who can't be trusted. But you'll probably be in good company with the brotha who never calls fouls and tries to get everyone involved.

3. "Remember, Listen to Aunt Tina (Turner). Love ain't got nothing to do with some shit." This includes (but isn't limited to):

A) If he puts his hands on you. Anytime somebody has to lay your ass out in order to show you that they love you, there's clearly something wrong with them. Bottom line, they don't love you if they have to thump you to show you. They just love the way their fists feel against your skin.

B) If he spends a ton of money on you. Money and love aint the same thing and shouldn't be construed otherwise. Some of the best loves were made of people of simple means, like Aladdin and Apu. Aladdin was broke as the fuck. Shit, he even had a whole song about being broke, but what they had was real.

C) If he just makes you feel better about yourself. To them, you could just be any random person. They could be your *Lucky Charms*, but to them, you might just be some low-fat, low-sugar, fiber-filled cereal. And, best believe, nobody likes that shit. Even the pigeons outside of hood bodegas thumb their noses at Food Club Lucky Charms.

D) If he loves sleeping with you (and vice versa). This just means that he loves to see you naked, and he's good at naked games.

4. "Calm the hell down sometimes. Seriously." You solve nothing by going ape-shit and overanalyzing every single email and/or text he sends you. And trust me, all men know that bitches love the smiley face. It's why Forrest Gump created them.

5. "Don't call him first all of the time." For one, he won't answer. For B, you're putting all of yours cards on the table by letting him know how pressed you are. The only thing that should be open 24/7 is 7-Eleven, and you ain't no convenience store, are you?

6. "'Keep dating." Just because you two met and hit it off doesn't mean that he's ready to bet the farm on you. In fact, most of us don't even have a farm to bet, so why in Sam Hill would we be ready to close up shop when we don't even own one? Think about that. It's deep. Don't get so caught up in that one dude that you forget to still see other people.

7. "Don't be Bob Costas." While it's understood that women generally need avenues to verbally emote, there's a fine line between *fishing for innocent feedback* and *scooping the salon with every salacious relationship specific like Sandra Rose.*

218

Your mom doesn't need to know about every minute disagreement you've ever had. And, if you actually want to keep your man from sleeping with one of your friends, your lonely ass girls don't need to be briefed with every bottom-line banality of your bi-weekly bedroom back-breakings. Remember that you're in a relationship with one person...not one-third of your blackberry's address book.

8. "Get a little ghost on occasion." Don't be so available. Make the guy feel like he's working for something. Get a hobby[77] besides checking Facebook every 15 minutes to see if he changed his status to *"In a relationship."*

9. "The peace is good. Try not to disturb it." Men lie. Despite this admittedly troubling fact, our white lies are one of our most chivalrous acts, our way of protecting you all from windmills, waterfalls, and our burgeoning porn addictions, and it's a relationship death knell to worry yourself over every minor inconsistency. Think about it:

---

[77] "Hobbies" definitely makes the cut when listing **"Underrated and Occasionally Overlooked Easy to Obtain Positive Attributes That Every Grown-Ass Sista Should Possess"** The rest?

1. Nice Hair. Whether you're rocking braids or a baldy, a bob or a Halle, deceiving weave or the "Spelman Pullback," a grown-ass sista should know **A)** How to handle your 'do and **B)** Which 'do is most appropriate for you.

2. A Go-To Dude. Every grown-ass sista should have at least one *heterosexual!* male in her life that'll give it to her straight with no chaser whenever she needs to know *"What does it mean when he says that he only wants to see me between 3:00 and 3:45am on the weekends?"* and other deep insights about the mysterious male mind. —*T.C.*

Do you really want us to tell you the truth about everything?[78]

10. "No man is worth fighting for." Read that statement very carefully, though. You can defend your man. In fact, you should defend your man if you ever see him in distress and are in a position to provide assistance. Thing is, *there are absolutely no circumstances where it's okay to fight another woman in order to win a man's affection.* No man is worth this. If it ever gets to this point, cut your losses and walk away. Any man that's actually worth fighting for wouldn't even let you have to fight to win his affection.

11. "Don't sleep with a man unless he's earned it." We know this sounds like heresy to our brothas out there, but let's just keep it 100. Plus, if a dude is mad because you didn't put it in 6 hours after your first date, he's probably not the cat for you anyway.

12. "Relax. There are enough men to go around for everyone." You're not a wrinkled shirt. Once again, we know the stats, but damn, there actually are men out there, and probably one for you.

So, realize every man isn't for you and let some of the crappy ones go, and don't worry about a "good" one being taken off of the market by your girl, a white woman, or his gay pastor. **Trust us, none of us—not even your daddy—is worth all of that.**

---

[78] When he says, *"Your cooking tastes just like my mother's,"* do you **really** need to know that he'd already be dead if his mother cooked anything like you do? Exactly. –*P.J.*

Why I Hate "Good Girl" Problems
A Very Smart Rant from Panama Jackson

Corn, guacamole, and chicks with fake lashes. Women who go out and purchase fake asses. Turbocharged Hyundais and big pinky rings. These are a few of my most hated things.

But, despite the fact that each of these things make my gums bleed, none of them draw my ire easier than "good girl" issues. Good girls, at their core, are really just women who don't want to come off as heathenistic hedonists, and there's really nothing wrong with that. But, what pisses me off about *them* is that they run amok amongst the rest of us secure individuals, polluting the dating world with odd rules and timetables intended to fool somebody into thinking that they don't have urges or don't like licking schlongs. Put more simply, **good girls are the biggest cockteases known to man.**

You remember that chick Helen...from Troy? Cocktease. Do you know why her face launched a thousand ships? Because Menelaus was mad that she was playing all coy with him, but was giving it up on the side to Paris even though she didn't love him. Or something like that. My Greek mythology is a little rusty, like your trombone if you're dealing with a *good* girl. Here are a couple more reasons why good girl issues infuriate me so.

1. The rules have absolutely no rhyme or reason. Do you remember how you weren't supposed to feed the Gremlins after midnight? That shit made total sense, especially once you saw what happened when Gizmo's kids got some after-hour snackage. On the flipside, *do not sleep with a guy for 90 days* has absolutely no fucking

221

purpose other than to allow a woman to say, *"I didn't sleep with him for 3 months so I'm not a ho."*

2. It's usually disingenuous. Most good girls are as sexually charged and hyper-intimate as the guys they're keeping on the bench, which wouldn't be a problem if they weren't such fucking asshole cockteases. You can't be out here making innuendo-ass comments and jokingly referencing what you'll do to somebody if you have precluded yourself from actually doing anything because of your inane-ass rules (see #1).

Basically, if you have to suppress who you are to make yourself look better, you're probably just a ho in sheep's clothing. Sleeping with people doesn't make you a ho. A woman can sleep with 100 men and not be considered a ho. Then again, you can have a chick who has boned 5 guys who's the biggest ho everybody knows. Basically, if you let me put it on your forehead because I asked, well you might be a ho. But, if you at least ask me to wipe off your forehead after I'm done, you just might be a classy lady.[79]

---

[79] **Extremely Naked (and extremely offensive) Dating Truth #122:** For **women**, true love is a pronoun, the final destination, a series of serendipitous events, a never-ending Telemundo novela where themes are always earth-toned and breezy, earnest and virile husbands promise their dying father-in-laws *"Yo siempre cuidará de la niña"*, and impeccably coiffed women lay on sheets of ostrich feathers while serenaded by the faint hum of a Santa Ana and the soft pedaled tune of choreographed orgasms. For **men**, true love is being asked not to cum in her hair the day after she got it done, and seriously considering the idea of respecting her wishes. −*T.C.*

The Cheat Sheet
"Secrets" About Men That We Can't (In Good Conscience) End the Book Without Telling You

By The Champ and Panama Jackson

As you may or may not already know, peeing while showering with your mate (*without splashing on each other*) is a tricky skill that takes much practice and preparation. The Champ and one of his ex's mastered this feat, basically becoming the Jedi Knights of shower urination. She even started calling him "Ace Windu"

Even if you think that this is "WTMI" (Waaaaaaay Too Much Information) or just extraordinarily disgusting, you have to appreciate and admire the sheer skill level this takes. Once, while they were showering and she was mid-pee, they heard her cell phone ringing on the bathroom sink. It was an important call that she had been expecting, so she stopped mid-pee, exited the shower and picked up the phone. He stood there literally awestruck, thinking to himself...

"Wow!!! Beautiful, smart, can cook, and she has the strongest vagina muscles on the planet. Damn, it's like I won the lottery."

After she returned to the shower, he felt the need to express what he'd been feeling.

"Wow. You have a gift down there."

"What are you talking about? I already said no sex right now, Champ, I'm tired."

223

"No, no, no, no, no. I'm talking about the way you stopped your pee so easily. We need to call the Guinness book or something. That was amazing."

"Champ, honey. Ummmm, I don't mean to burst your bubble, but all women can stop their urine easily. It's nothing. Wait...men can't stop their pee???"

To answer her question: No we can't. Wait, that's a lie. Technically we can, but it's very, very, very, very, very, very difficult for us to do, and should only be attempted in extreme *"Damn, here comes the mother-in-law. I sure picked a horrible time to water her flowers"* types of situations.

Anyway, assuming that *surprisingly graphic male urinary habits* weren't exactly what you had in mind when seeing the title of this chapter, here are a few more gems that should accelerate your journey to Very Smartness.

1. Every (yup, *every*) man in a romantic relationship has a mistress. Sometimes it's an ex-girlfriend we've kept in contact with because we know she's always only one word from go. Sometimes it's a co-worker we share so many inside jokes and lunch runs with that we *almost* don't mind it when the Chili's waitress assumes we're not splitting the check. Sometimes it's the cute barista at our favorite Starbucks we always exchange *"I'm probably a bit happier to see you than I should be"* smiles with. And sometimes, well, sometimes that mistress might just be our mom.

You see, regardless of status or station, pretty much every man has at least one source of validation in his life **outside of his significant other** that reminds him of how attractive, funny, and unique he is; a perpetually legitimizing force—a person who thinks we're the shit, laughs at each of our corny jokes, and doesn't remind us that we've told them that story three times already—we don't have any interest in actually sleeping with.

In theory, we should get this validation from our *real* relationships. And, in theory, we actually do. Girlfriends and wives are the shit (mostly). But, although knowing that your significant other still finds you somewhat attractive is all that *counts*, it's not all that *matters*. The need to know that we're still interesting and desirable to others dissipates but never disappears.

And, what separates us from women is the fact that while most women can't walk a block and a half without someone letting them know they're still desirable in someway, most men don't have this same luxury. This is where the mistress steps in, providing a breezy recess session for our psyches; an admittedly superficial reminder of who we think we are when we look in the mirror after our morning push-ups puff our chests.

2. If we're serious about you, our anxiety about meeting your mom has nothing to do with "*Will I get along with her*" and everything to do with "*So that's what she's probably going to look like in 25 years.*" While this isn't exactly fair (and might not even be useful), most men have been taught by other, older men to use the mother as a gage for how the daughter will eventually look. Usually these wise older men are found at basketball courts, in barbershop shops, and outside of liquor stores, but that's beside the point.

Anyway, this is especially true with thicker, curvier women, whose men will look to their mothers for visual confirmation of how thick his chick will eventually get. I'm telling you, one of the scariest things a man could ever see is an old picture of your "Big Momma" sized mom that shows how hot and *eerily similar to you* she looked back in the day.

This is why every woman thinking about marrying a guy should buy her mom a Bally's membership before letting Mom Dukes meet him. If that doesn't work, just make sure you hide every picture of her that was taken before 1990.

3. We already know whether or not you came. We just ask afterwards because it makes us all warm and fuzzy inside when you say it. Even if we already know that you did, there's no bigger ego boost than hearing verbal confirmation of it. It's like what happens when you get your first real adult paycheck, and you check your bank balance every four hours just to see it. You know its still there, but you can never tire of the feeling of actually seeing it jump out at you from the ATM receipt.

Also, other than *"Are you okay?"* and *"I'll be right back. I'm going to go buy and make breakfast"* we don't say a word afterwards if we know you didn't climax. Since we're feeling like we're treading on thin ice, this is also probably the best time to ask him for favor such as a ride to the airport at 6 am on a week day or a new car.

4. No, those weren't tears in our eyes at the end of *The Notebook*. We just have allergies and shit sometimes. We also caught allergies at the end of *Akeelah and the Bee*, and while watching the end of The Roots "You Got

226

Me" video, and this is all purely coincidental, and none of the symptoms of these mysterious allergies should ever be made public.

5. Us being "excited" when you're wearing sexy lingerie has less to do with how you look in it than the fact that we know we're about to get some. We appreciate the effort though. It doesn't matter if you're wearing the latest line from Victoria's Secret or the jogging set you bought at Mafia Sweat Suits 'R' Us, we're still just as excited to see you. It'll all end up in a ball in our mouths or beside our beds anyway. With that being said, we'll continue to purchase outrageously priced underwear for you because we know that it makes you feel sexier when you're wearing it, and you feeling sexier means good feelings for everybody and (wait for it) **less crime.**

6. Most of us will never admit this freely, but much of what we do which falls under the "done to impress women" category is done solely to impress *other men.* It's common knowledge that women do certain things (i.e.: *French manicures, purchasing outrageously priced purses, etc*) knowing that the only people who will probably notice it is will be other women. What isn't so common knowledge is the fact that most men partake in this same practice, but, because of a fear of appearing less manly, we will never admit it. We're not talking about hot-dog eating or farting contests either, but stuff we regularly do under the guise of *impressing women.*

For instance, in college The Champ probably owned at least 50 to 60 pairs of sneakers, especially higher-end basketball shoes such as Air Jordans. Sometimes he wouldn't even take them out of the shoeboxes for months, just stacking them on the wall next to his dresser, occasionally brushing the dust off the top of the box just to be pretentious. Although he spent a considerable amount of money and time to keep his shoe collection up, most of the women he knew and were interested in could care less about his damn Jordans. Most of the compliments and appreciation he'd receive about the shoes were from *other guys*, and, even though it's taboo for a straight guy to admit this, he valued that even more than some chick telling him he had nice kicks.

Ironically, the guys who **do** dress in a way to try to attract women (i.e.: *form fitting skinny jeans, sleeveless turtlenecks, etc)* are the ones whose style is more likely to be referred to as "**gay**" by other guys. Go figure.

7. We fake it too. Women do not have sole ownership claim to the *fake an orgasm* thing. There at times where we may be too tired or too distracted or too drunk to complete the mission. But, because we're too embarrassed to let the woman know that we're just not up to it (and because we know that telling the truth will probably hurt the woman's feelings as well), we'll give ourselves an out. Plus, if it's protected sex, there's going to be no proof of our deception. I mean, how often do (sane) women actually check the old condom to see if there's anything in there?

8. There are more than a few "woman-ish" things we like much, much more than we want you to think we do. These include (but aren't limited to):

A) Gossip. Although most men probably don't have websites like Bossip and TMZ bookmarked and probably won't spend an afternoon in a Gmail group chat with our homeboys about why we're hurt that D-Money didn't tell us about his new Jamaican jump-off, we're just as prone to the gossip bug as the typical woman is. Don't believe me? Well, go to any barbershop and listen in while we discuss the *real reason* why Jay-Z and Dame Dash don't get along anymore or which saleslady at the Foot Locker across the street looks like she gives the best head. Still not convinced? Take a trip over to ESPN.com and read the endless thousand comment threads devoted to Shaq and Kevin Garnett's first synchronized chest bump as teammates.

B) Commitment. Most men aren't scared of commitment, and we actually welcome it. We're just scared to death of committing to the wrong person. Big difference.

C) Shopping. Whether it's shoes, cars, stereo equipment, gas grills, or pussy, we like new shit just as much as everyone else, and we don't mind making a trip to a place to purchase what we want. It's just that we loathe the concept of shopping as a group and/or all-day activity, which is a diplomatic way of saying "*We hate shopping with women.*"

D) Cuddling. We all love the cuddle. It keeps us warm, reminds us of how good you smell, and helps us honor our sandbox tenet to do what we can to get as many cheap feels per day as possible.

9. It actually does hurt us when you cry. Also, if you want to elicit sympathy from us in an argument, remember that faux sadness works much, much, much better than faux anger.

10. Your taste in music generally makes us want to stab midgets and squirrels.[80] For the life of us, we can't understand how you all manage to even listen to some of the auditory disasters you all call your favorite music. This is actually one of the reasons why we were so adamant earlier in the book about lack of good taste in music being a potential deal-maker. For most men, finding a woman who actually can expand his music horizons is like finding a virgin at an abortion rally. We know they exist, but we also won't be holding our breath until we discover one. We still love you, though. Just don't be surprised if we "accidentally" drop your iPod in the toilet the next time you leave it laying on the coffee table.

11. If we seriously desired that your boobs were bigger or your ass was fatter, we would just find somebody with bigger boobs or a fatter ass. As we've alluded to many times in this book, we're aware of how neurotic women can be about their looks, and we know that this neurosis is (partially) our fault. Thing is, the visual nature of men always has to be considered. Basically, since we're the ones who approached you, we were pleased with what you brought to the table before we even knew what your name was and there's really no need to obsess about this. If we weren't pleased, we would have stayed our asses across the bar instead of trekking through 30 feet of

---

[80] Seriously, though. The terrible taste in movies and music thing is one of those phenomena we don't understand. I mean, how can an entire gender full of extremely intelligent and intuitive people have such consistently bad taste when it comes to performance art? How many more Netflix nights watching *Why Did I Get Married* with you do we need to suffer through before we start a *"Help! My girlfriend always picks terrible movies on Netflix and I can't do anything about it"* Facebook group? —*T.C.*

drunk hoodrats, armed thugs, and club smoke just to say "Hi."

Basically, if we're with you, we love how you look (unless, of course, you decided to become Ike Austin).

12. There are more than a few things that you obsess over that most guys could really give two shits about. This list includes:

A) Saggy boobs. While it's safe to say that men probably aren't going to go gaga if your boobs look like you've duct taped two deflated water balloons to your chest, we realize that boobs (especially big boobs) tend to sag and we're perfectly okay with that. In fact, it's actually kind of hot to take off a woman's bra and watch her boobs fall and sprint out of that bitch like Usain Bolt.

B) Stretch marks. You're good, as long as they're not on your forehead.

C) How soon you've given *it* up. While it is true that a guy's opinion of you might change if you don't wait until a *suitable* (*and, remember, "suitable" is completely arbitrary*) time has passed before deciding to sleep with him, **this only makes a difference if he wasn't really that into in the first place** and is basically just looking for a reason to eliminate you. If he really likes you, it won't matter if you slept with him after four great dates or four great *days*, he's still going to think just as highly of you afterward.

D) How much you eat. It amazes me to hear about a grown-ass woman ordering Caesar salads and ice water and shit on her first date, only to have to cut it short

231

because her stomach is growling so loudly that it seems like a family of pit bulls are living inside of her. Granted, when the menu comes, it's probably not a good look to tell the waiter *"Yeah, just gimme page 2,"* but if we wanted to date someone who looked and ate like a six year old boy we would have been Catholic priests.

E) Gifts. Although we love gifts as much as anyone else, our love for them is more *"Cool. New shit"* than *"Wow! She really must have taken a lot of time to think about this."* The thought doesn't count any more than a Target gift card does.

F) Whether your expert-level bedroom prowess will scare us away. To paraphrase Katt Williams—our favorite black baby-haired midget pimp comedian—never in the history of niggadom has a nigga slept with his chick and thought to himself, *"Damn! She's a freak! I had no idea a wet elbow could do so many things. She's so freaky in fact that she must have actually had sex with someone else before she met me. Since that's probably true, I can't continue to date her."*

G) Your hair anywhere other than the top of your head. Again, while having legs that feel like brown sugar cactuses when they're laying next to you isn't what's hot in the streets, obsessing to the point of neurosis over your eyebrows, eyelashes, armpits, and pubic area just makes us think you're even crazier than we already think you are.

H) What it smells like *down there*. As long as it doesn't seem like you've been spraying "Sex Panther" by Odeon between your legs, you have nothing to be self-conscious about. Actually, we all love what that thing smell like, word to Black Jesus.

I) Whether we'll be upset that your jeans are Target brand instead of True Religion. There's actually a word for guys who really care about stuff like that, and it starts with "h" and rhymes with "logofexual."

K) Your age. I'm not going to say that age doesn't matter, but most guys are more concerned with how old a woman *looks* and *acts* than how old she actually *is*. We'd much rather be with an active and youthful 37 year old than a 25 year old who looks like she lived through and slept with the Great Depression.

13. For your own benefit, you should probably know that there's literally nothing that you can do to make a guy who wants to stray stay. Basically, a man at the end of the relationship is like an iceberg. You might only see the tip—*the seemingly out of nowhere break-up talk*—but rest assured that there's a couple tons of ice lurking beneath the surface. He's wanted to break up for a while, and he just now grew enough balls to actually tell you. Nothing, not even a promise of copious and frequent sex, can "*win*" a man back, so don't even try.

14. "A woman's life is love; a man's love is life..." This line, uttered by Phonte of Little Brother/Foreign Exchange on "Breakin' My Heart," might be the most poignant utterance in the history of utterances. Sometimes, women spend so much time trying to find love that they can't understand why men don't feel the same way, forgetting that, for most men, love is just another part of life; not the end-all-be-all of life itself.

15. Until we say "I love you" without you prompting it, we don't. You'll know a man loves you when he just can't stop himself from telling you. If you ask a man if he loves you, and he says, "Yes," he still hasn't technically said it, he just answered the question that creates the shortest distance between your mouth and his schlong.

16. Actions speak louder than words. But unless he says the words, don't go assuming anything. Basically, don't ever assume he's your man, without first having one of those "*Wait, man. So are you my boyfriend or not?*" conversations. More simply, if we never say I love you or that you're our girlfriend, we don't and you aren't.

17. The reason why some of us use lazy and obnoxious pick-up lines as our only ways to approach women? They (occasionally) work. Scenario: Let's say Panama and your typical boneheaded and lascivious youngster, who "Hey baby" and "pssssst" at everything walking, both go to the mall to buy some slacks and pick up chicks. Panama sees his potential pick-up (and a group of her friends) in The Gap and lays out an impromptu plan of attack for approach:

Hmmmm, okay. She's with her girls now so I'll have to, in essence, impress all of them just to get some rhythm from her. Okay...this might work. I'll walk up to them and tell them that I'm trying to find a pair of capris for my mom, and that I need help. If they're good people, they'll happily oblige. When they ask me what size pants my mother would wear, I'll feign ignorance at first, pretending to be completely inexperienced with figuring women's sizes. Then, I'll pretend to have an epiphany and nod towards the woman that I'm interested in, remarking, "she's actually about your size." At that point she'll hopefully take the lead...maybe even leading me around the store to look at stuff she thinks my mom would like. This is when it's time for me to work my magic, reading her reactions to my self-deprecating yet strangely confident demeanor, subtlety creating a spark in the short time we have left. She probably knows that the whole "mom" thing was just a pick-up approach, but she'll probably appreciate the effort and continue to "play along" until I up the ante.

Seems like a lot of trouble just to get a phone number from some random woman, who might not even be interested in you, right? Yes, you're definitely right. It is a ton of work, but it's also what every *considerate* or *smooth* man has to do to get some type of rhythm in a situation like that. The odds are that a cold approach, even if the girl you're approaching is interested, will probably amount to nothing. Plus, as Panama mentioned in Chapter 2, her girls have the power to summon all of the testes-blocking power on the planet to thwart your effort with just a simple expertly placed eye roll or sucking of teeth. To be able to do what you want to do you need to disarm them, profess interest in something other than an ass-waist ratio even if the ass-waist ratio is all you really care about, and find a way to isolate yourself with the potential so that you have at least 80 seconds of conversation time by yourselves.

That entire process (thinking of and implementing the plan) might take five to ten minutes. Lots of work for one freakin' phone number, right?

Now, remember the *typical boneheaded and lascivious youngster* who whistles and hollers at everything walking is also at the mall. In the 10 minutes Panama spent planning and implementing his approach, the other cat

235

has already hollered at 15 different women, getting two phone numbers in the process. Although his *bagging percentage* will be much lower than P's, he managed to get twice the results with only half the effort.

The point of this longwinded exposition is that it's easier to just say some nonsense at any random woman you find attractive. Even though you'll look like an idiot, it takes less effort but occasionally produces equal results. Sure, the quality might not be the same, but quantity has a way of making things seem better. Plus, it can get a bit draining mentally to continuously plan approaches. It's so hard out here for a considerate pimp.

18. All we really want to do is make you happy. But, we need your help to do so.

Think about it: With all the shit you all have going on in your heads, do you even really want us to be able to read your minds? We thought so.

Acknowledgements

This book would be 300 pages long if we attempted to acknowledge everyone who helped us along this Very Smart journey. But, along with our awesome parents, families, friends, and fans, we can't write another word without giving due to the lovely and incomparable Liz Burr, who apparently was born with an almost godly reservoir of patience to help her put up with our daily nonsense.

Also, if you don't already know, we'd like to inform you that Sarah Huny Young is the shit. God is too.

Lastly, we imagine there will be more than a few people reading *Your Degrees Won't Keep You Warm at Night* who will suspect that a particular chapter or passage was inspired by them. Some of these people will be correct.

If you happen to be one of these correct people, thank you!!! Or, if "sorry" would be more appropriate, sorry.